VEGAN MEALS
FOR ONE OR TWO

Also by Nancy Berkoff, RD

Vegan in Volume – Vegan Quantity Recipes for Every Occasion

Dedication

Vegan Meals for One or Two is dedicated to Bob, my heart, the love of my life, and source of all my inspiration and strength. Thank you for your insight, your warmth, and your depth. Thank you for being the source of all things wonderful.

VEGAN MEALS
FOR ONE OR TWO

Your Own Personal Recipes

By Chef Nancy Berkoff, RD

The Vegetarian Resource Group
Baltimore, Maryland

A NOTE TO THE READER

The contents of *Vegan Meals for One or Two* are not intended to provide personal medical advice. Medical advice should be obtained from a qualified health professional.

© Copyright 2001, The Vegetarian Resource Group
PO Box 1463, Baltimore, MD 21203.

Cover artwork by Lance Simons
Illustrations by Rowen Leigh

Library of Congress Cataloging-in-Publication Data
Vegan Meals for One or Two – Your own Personal Recipes/
Nancy Berkoff
Library of Congress Catalog Card Number: 2001130420

ISBN 0-931411-23-8

Printed in the United States of America

10 9 8 7 6 5 4 3 2 1

Table of Contents

Chapter 1   **It's all about You!** 8
Why this Book?.................................8
Vegan Nutrition.................................9
Healthy Living.................................13
About the Recipes 15
Several Words about Purchasing
     Ingredients...............................17
Stocking the Shelves..........................18
A Place for Everything and Everything
     in its Place (or Wash Your Hands
     and Keep it Clean)..........................19
Preparing Meals for One or Two 21

Chapter 2   **Meal Planning and Shopping** 22
Vegan Meal Planning 23
Sample Menu 25
Shopping and Stocking 26
Tools of the Trade.............................31
Kitchen Safety 32

Chapter 3   **Breakfast**....................................34
Items to Have on Hand 35
Some Fast Ideas to Get You Started........37
Breakfast Recipes.............................38

Chapter 4   **One-Pot Wonders**.........................56
Build a Meal in One Pot 57
One-Pot Recipes..............................59

Chapter 5   **Freeze or Refrigerate Now,**
Eat Later..86
Recipes You Can Freeze 88
Make Now, Use for the Week –
    Recipes You Can Refrigerate...........100

Chapter 6   **Grab-and-Go**................................113
Grab-and-Go Combinations Using
    Leftovers.......................................114
Grab-and-Go Entrées 118
Hot Beverage Recipes......................128
Cold Beverage Recipes......................133

Chapter 7   **Desserts and Snacks**...................140
Dessert Recipes 142
Snack Recipes 153

Chapter 8   **Every Day and Special Day**
Cooking 163
Entrée Recipes..................................166
Put on the Barbecue or Light up the
    Hibachi? Here are Some Ideas.........181

Glossary   Definitions of Vegan Products and
    Details on Less Common Cooking
    Terms or Products...........................188
Measurements 189
Soy Substitutes 192

Resources from The Vegetarian
Resource Group...........................195

Index....................................203

Preface

In this frazzled, not-enough-time-for-the-important-stuff world, we can still take comfort in the warmth and coziness of our kitchens. The kitchen can be the last bastion of nurturing and refuge.

Vegan Meals for One or Two was born with that in mind. Eating over the sink or popping a cup-of-soup into the microwave is not the way to reward yourself. Nor is it the best way to keep yourself healthy and feeling up to the challenges of life. You will find tasty, healthy, and pampering recipes in this book.

There have always been diet and eating trends. Today, there are several very popular diets that encourage meals based on very high protein intakes, with the majority of protein coming from animal sources. Not only are these diets destructive to the humans who are ingesting them, they are inhumane for the animals forced to provide the meal. Certainly there may be weight loss on these diets. However, there may be increased blood cholesterol levels with the ensuing heightened blood pressure and blocked arteries, and the danger of heart disease, diabetes, and other diseases related to diets high in animal fats.

Vegan Meals for One or Two suggests a way to save the planet, be kind to animals, and save yourself at the same time. Not too bad a deal – indulgent food, healthy feelings, and living the good and ethical life, with nary a sacrifice for your palate.

Many thanks to Debra Wasserman and Charles Stahler who encouraged the writing of this book and provided hours of assistance, enthusiasm, and all-around cheerleading. Without their support and guidance, this book would be a project still in the planning stage. Also, thank you for making me part of the VRG family and providing life-examples that inspire.

Finally, special thanks to Sarah Ellis, RD, for providing the nutritional analyses for the recipes, Lance Simons for designing the cover, Rowen Leigh for doing the illustrations, and to the following VRG volunteers who proofread parts of the manuscript and offered valuable advice: Amy Bottrell, Jennifer Femia, W.H. (Dell) Lunceford, Susan Petrie, Sheri Runtsch, Stephanie Schueler, William P. Tandy, and Susan Weinstein.

– Nancy Berkoff. RD

Chapter One

It's all about You!

Everyone wants to feel and look good. You can't escape that old adage "you are what you eat." What would you rather "be" – fresh berries, crisp carrots, and aromatic rice or cholesterol, refined sugar, and pork fat? We bet we know your answer!

Eating vegan is a lifestyle choice that will enhance your life. With this book, you'll find vegan cooking and eating easy. Each recipe is written to serve one or two people, so no more excuses. We've heard the "but I'm the only one in my family who's eating vegan meals" excuse, the "I'm vegan, but it's so hard to cook for one, so I mostly do the fast food thing" excuse, and even the "you can't cook vegan food for just one" excuse. None of these excuses are valid anymore. You have no good reason to eat unhealthy, eat non-vegan, and not start a good thing for yourself. Do the research – you'll find few diabetic, hypertensive, low-energy vegans. Who knows, you might start feeling better, have more energy, have some of your physical complaints disappear, and start feeling better about yourself. At the same time you'll be doing something good for the planet.

Why this Book?

Professional chefs and amateur cooks know that it's a lot easier to cook for a crowd than for one or two people, unless you're really, really into leftovers. When we cook for ourselves (and that's more "if" than "when") we tend to blow the dust off the stuff in the back of the refrigerator and heat it up. Many of us don't take the time to treat ourselves well. There's nothing wrong with an occasional Cheerios and banana dinner (or leftover cold pizza breakfast), but you deserve better than that. With a little planning and a little dedication, your kitchen can become more than a room to nuke coffee, and your refrigerator will become more than a haven for alien life forms.

Are we promising elegant banquets for one or two and no leftovers? The answer is yes and no. Many of the recipes will yield elegant banquets (the ambiance is your responsibility). Most of the recipes will yield two hearty portions, so there may be leftovers. But not I've-got-to-eat-Brussels-sprouts-for-two-weeks kind of leftovers, just a portion or two. We've tried to design recipes that realistically use ingredients the way they come packaged in the store. The recipes allow you to decide what types of dishes you'll want to make in larger amounts and which dishes you won't make in large amounts. For example, salsa and muffins can be made in larger portions than a tofu scramble. In other words, items that will hold up for several days, require more effort to make, or have multiple uses, have larger recipe yields than one-meal-is-enough items.

Vegan is the thinking-person's choice. No more fast food mentalities here. If you are what you eat, and your body will only perform as well as the fuel you stoke it with, than eating a well-thought out vegan diet may be the key to your happiness and success.

Vegan Nutrition

We have written this book with the understanding that a vegan refrains from eating meat, fish, poultry, eggs, dairy, honey, etc. In other words, there are no animals or animal byproducts.

A vegan diet is like any other type of diet. Variety is the key. Just as someone who lives at Burger King is probably not getting a balance of nutrients, the same can be said for someone who eats mostly rice and broccoli. There are lots of good foods out there; be sure you are including them every day. Chapter 2 offers a vegan menu-planning guide to help balance your menu.

When people speak about "vegan nutrition issues," they are usually speaking about the amount of protein, iron, calcium, and vitamin B12 found in the diet. Protein is easy; if you eat a varied diet with an adequate amount of calories, you'll probably take in enough protein. Up until several years ago, protein planning or protein combining was thought to be essential. The two-minute explanation of this is as follows: essential amino acids, found in proteins, are necessary for growth and repair of tissues and muscles, important for the formation and maintenance of a healthy immune system, etc. Animal proteins contain all the essential amino acids. Plant proteins contain all of the essential amino acids but in different proportions than are found in animal proteins. It was thought that you conscientiously had to combine plant foods, such as rice and beans or lentils and pasta, in order to guarantee the intake of complete proteins. We now know that as long as you eat lots of different foods each day, by hook or by crook, you'll have the proper amino acid intake. So, don't live just on apples and broccoli – throw in some soymilk, hummus, or a bean burrito, too. By the way, soy products have essential amino acids in proportions similar to those in animal proteins. If you have days when you know that you're just not going to be able to vary your diet, try to include some soymilk, edamame (look it up in the glossary!), tofu, or a soy burger.

Iron and vitamin C really like each other. In fact, when you eat iron and vitamin C containing foods, your body is able to absorb more iron than it would if vitamin C wasn't around. You may know the vitamin C containing foods: oranges, grapefruit, tangerines and their juices, kiwi, strawberries, tomatoes, peppers and chilies, mangos and papayas, and green veggies. So, can you name at least ten foods containing iron? Here are some: lentils, black-eyed peas, soybeans, raisins and prunes, all kinds of greens (mustard, kale, beet, chard, spinach, etc.), blackstrap molasses, black beans, watermelon, garbanzo beans, seitan, tempeh, and iron-enriched cereals and grain products. With that type of variety, you should have no problem consuming adequate iron and vitamin C.

Many of the foods that contain iron also contain calcium, including greens, vegetables (like broccoli and bok choy), blackstrap molasses, and tofu. Look for tofu processed with calcium sulfate, as this is a good source of calcium. Vegan milks can be fortified with calcium, so select brands that offer this. The same goes for products made with vegan milks, such as soy cheeses and convenience items (like frozen entrées). Nuts and seeds can be a modest source of calcium (just for perspective, 1/2 cup of firm tofu has about 300 milligrams of calcium and 1/4 cup of almonds has about 90 milligrams). Sneak in calcium wherever you can – use a fortified soymilk for your coffee, add calcium-processed tofu to your salad dressing, and toss some chopped walnuts and sesame seeds in your salad.

Vitamin B12 is an important vitamin for red blood cell health. The daily requirement is very low and vegans can obtain vitamin B12 from fortified products, such as some cold breakfast cereals and vegan milks. Be sure to read the labels! Nutritional yeast (see the glossary for more details) may be fortified with vitamin B12. Red Star Company has a nutritional yeast product formulated for vegans called Vegetarian Support Formula. Nutritional yeast has a cheezy flavor and can be sprinkled on cereal, blended into smoothies, and added to baking recipes, salad dressings, soups, and stir-fries.

So, what about cholesterol and fat? The good news is that vegan diets should have no cholesterol, as cholesterol is found in animal products. Saturated fats are found in animal products and this type of fat appears to be even more harmful than cholesterol. Coconut oil, palm oil, and some margarines are high in saturated fat. Do you have to eliminate them? This depends on your health status, the amount of saturated fat you eat, and your family history. If you are healthy, an occasional bit of coconut oil is not going to cause major problems.

Unsaturated fats are considered to do less damage and may have some health benefits. Olive oil and olives, avocado, vegetable oils (corn, safflower, cottonseed, soy, etc.), and nuts and seeds are all examples of foods high in unsaturated fats and oils. Some people add grapeseed oil, primrose oil, or flaxseed oil to their cooking, as they feel these oils have some health benefits. You'll have to do some reading on this topic if this interests you. Remember, according to the US Dietary Guidelines, your daily calories from fat should be less than thirty percent. The American Heart Association would like you to get your daily calories from fat down to less than or equal to thirty percent also. This means if you eat about 2000 calories, you have about 600 fat calories to play around with.

To give you some reference, any one of the following contain about 50 calories of fat:

1-1/4 teaspoons of vegetable oil (any type, because oil is oil when it comes to calories), about 8 ripe olives, 1-1/2 teaspoons solid margarine, or 1/8 of an avocado.

Why this discussion about fat? Because, even though humans require a certain amount of fat in their diet to help with the metabolism of vitamins and minerals and to maintain health, we tend to overdo fat intake. Hey, it's an easy way to make foods moist and to add flavor, but overindulgence in fat calories has been linked to heart disease, diabetes, and certain cancers. Who needs that? There are other ways to get juiciness and flavor on your plate. Sautéing in a bit of vegetable broth, using vegetable oil spray rather than stick margarine for cooking, and tossing veggies with spices and herbed vinegar are just some of the ways to have a flavorful meal with less fat. Just look at what and how you eat and evaluate your fat intake accordingly. We are not telling you to skip the peanut butter, avocado, or tempura; we're just recommending a little moderation. Some people are very good at balance, but some of us give into the "well, I'm not eating steak or butter, so I can do more frying" routine. Vegan diets can be inherently low fat, with the accent on grains, fruit, vegetables, beans, and soy products. Just pace yourself. Yes, an order of fries and a green salad with oil and vinegar dressing may be a fast food vegan option, but it's not what you want to do very often.

So, if you cut out some of the fat, do you cut out some of the fun? Don't be silly! Garlic and lemon grilled portobello mushrooms, basil tomato stuffed eggplant, baby greens salad with raspberries, walnuts, and oranges, curried carrot soup, and gingered pumpkin sorbet are all low fat and taste very good (and they're vegan). Whaddaya think? Can you do it? We think so!

Healthy Living

Here are some ideas to think about when you are shopping and preparing your meals:

- Add canned beans (including soybeans) to soups, pastas, pizzas, and stews.

- Mix edamame (fresh, cooked soybeans, available frozen) into green salads and pasta salads; eat them as a snack instead of chips, or use them as a hot or cold side dish.

- Alternate peanut butter with soy butter, hazelnut butter, and almond butter.

- Flavor soups and stews with miso, puréed vegetables, and nutritional yeast to increase the soy, vitamins, and minerals in your meals.

- Check out soy "coffee cream" as another way to add soy to your menu.

- Add nuts and dried fruit to muffin and quick bread batters, rice, couscous, and barley.

- Thinly grate raw beets, carrots, jicama, and other root veggies and add these to salads and soups.

- Remember lower fat cooking techniques include steaming, poaching, barbecuing, wok-cooking, broiling, baking, and roasting; use vegetable and fruit juice, vegetable or mushroom broth, and wine as a cooking liquid, rather than always using oil or margarine. Not only will this cut down on fat; it will create new taste sensations!

- All fruit is good, and some are great! A food science professor at Rutgers University went looking for fruit that contained at least eight important vitamins and minerals per 3-ounce serving. He found that kiwi, papaya, cantaloupe, strawberries, mangoes, lemons, oranges, and avocados fit the bill. Walnuts and Brazil nuts, carrots, sweet potatoes, and broccoli were pretty high up there in nutrient density, too, with lots of vitamins and minerals.

- Add nuts to sauces, salads, cooked grains, vegetable dips, pancake batter, etc. Yes, nuts are higher in calories than many foods, but their fat is unsaturated and thought to offer many health benefits. Chop nuts and roll tofu, seitan, or tempeh in them and than bake for a crusted entrée. Purée pine nuts with basil and olive oil to make a fast pesto sauce for pasta or veggies.

- Think pasta. Pasta is low calorie (about 100 calories per 1/2 cup serving), high in complex carbohydrates, low in fat and sodium, and generally is fortified with folic acid, niacin, ribo-flavin, and iron. Pasta is fast to prepare, stores well, and it tastes good! If you're really in a hurry, have fresh pasta in your refrigerator. After the water boils, it takes only about 2-3 minutes to cook.

- Vitamin B12 is your buddy. Vegan sources of vitamin B12 are some fortified cold cereals, Red Star's Vegetarian Support Formula nutritional yeast, some fortified soy products (such as soymilk and meat analogs), and some ready-to-eat canned and frozen vegan products, such as veggie burgers.

When it comes to nutrition, your stomach doesn't distinguish what time of the day it is. Who of us hasn't had a bowl of corn-flakes for dinner or a cold burrito for breakfast? It's not the chronology, it's the balance. Add some kiwi, tomato, and pine-apple slices to that morning burrito and throw together a fruit smoothie to have with cereal (and toss some nuts into the cereal or have a half a bagel with peanut butter alongside it). Remem-ber, you're dedicated to balance and variety in your life and on your menu.

Kids swap items from their lunch boxes, so why shouldn't you? Veggies and non-veggies alike know that the sandwich is always better from someone else's knapsack. Form a lunch club; you bring appetizers one day and dessert the next. You don't have to be vegan to enjoy hummus and crunchy veggies, falafel in pita, veggie bean chili with cornbread, mushroom burgers with "the works," or lemon-poppy seed muffins (and yes, they can be made without eggs; substitute 1 Tablespoon of puréed firm tofu for each medium egg). Breaking bread together at school or work will tempt your taste buds and perhaps help to form great working relationships or friendships.

About the Recipes

All the recipes in this book are designed for two hearty servings, unless noted otherwise. Chapter 5 (Freeze or Refrigerate Now, Eat Later) has larger recipes, as these foods hold up to storage well. Some sauce or salad recipes may also make more than two servings, as they are versatile and can be used at several meals without becoming boring.

All recipes are vegan, so when we refer to "milk," we mean soy, rice, grain, or almond milk; "cheese" would be vegan soy cheese, etc. Since many vegans exclude refined white sugar and there are many varieties of unrefined sugar, we have written "dry sweetener" when we mean white sugar-type sweetener. Please see the glossary for more information on dry sweeteners. When you see "mayonnaise" listed, we mean vegan mayonnaise, which can be purchased or prepared at home (see the glossary for a vegan mayonnaise recipe).

We have attempted to keep the use of "specialty" items to a minimum, as they may not be available in your area or may not fit into your budget or cooking plans. If you keep a supply of tofu and vegan milk on hand you'll be able to prepare most of the recipes.

Use you imagination with the recipes. Remember, great chefs consider recipes just a guide. Utilize seasonal fruit and vege-tables, leftovers, and what's on sale at the store to replace some of the ingredients. For example, if red bell peppers are a better deal than green peppers this week, go for it. If you have leftover cooked barley, use it instead of the rice called for in a soup recipe. You get the idea.

Here's a word about garlic. Garlic is an easy and fast sea-soning, and a good base for other seasonings. Fresh garlic can be chopped clove by clove or you can purchase fresh garlic already chopped (this is sold in jars and must be kept refrigerated; it has a shell-life of about 2 weeks). If you don't think you'll use fresh garlic up before it starts sprouting, then purchase dry granulated garlic. It keeps for a long time and has more flavor than garlic powder. We don't like to use garlic salt (or for that matter onion or celery salt) as most people are trying to figure out ways to limit the amount of sodium they eat, and you don't need it in the seasoning anyway.

All the recipes in this cookbook are made with vegan ingredients, which means we have not used honey, eggs, or cheese. When possible, we have given you alternates for less-used ingredients. For example, whole bran, molasses, or dried orange zest may not be regular staples in your kitchen. You will see different alternates for different recipes, as we needed to consider textures, ingredient interaction, etc.

All recipes, unless noted, are mildly spiced. We figure you can always add more heat if you like, but you can't take it out. So go ahead and add twice as much fresh chili or use habañero chilies instead of bell pepper (remember, the remedy for chili mouth burn is milk or bread, not water). And please be careful when handling fresh chilies. Never touch your eyes or your face when you've been near chili seeds; the results are painful. Remember pepper spray is a weapon – where do you think they get the pepper from?

Several Words about Purchasing Ingredients

When you go shopping be realistic about what you will and won't use. We know that we get virtuous sometimes and buy enough fresh produce to have our own farmhouse buffet. A good rule of thumb is "will I (fill in the blank) prepare this, eat this, or like this the next three days?" If not, leave it on the shelf for the next consumer.

Be a label reader before you buy. You will, of course, be checking for vegan content. Also consider nutrient content. For example, if one orange juice has added calcium and one does not, go for the calcium. That makes one less nutrient you'll have to think about during the day. Also look at package directions. See if you have the time, patience, or equipment to prepare the product correctly. For example, if the directions state that a particular product has to be fried, it's a good bet that baking or microwaving won't work. We know this from personal experience. One of our friends destroyed a perfectly good microwave (and several veggie burgers). The directions for the burgers instructed that they were to be pan-fried. Instead, he decided to spray the frozen burgers with vegetable oil spray and microwave them (on high, of course). We had an appropriate burial for the microwave. That was two years ago, and his kitchen still smells like charred vegetables and melted plastic.

The following are some words that vegans don't want to see on a label, as they indicate the presence of animal products:

rennet, enzymes (have to verify the source; some are animal and some are vegetable), whey, casein, omega-3 fatty acids (usually from fish oil), natural casings, lactose, gelatin, gel, sucrose, tallow, albumin, etc.

Convenience sometimes wins. Get familiar with vegan convenience products available in your area. Canned soups, vegetables, and fruit, pre-chopped nuts, frozen vegetables and fruit, frozen or canned sauces, baking and pudding mixes, and pre-cut salads are convenience ingredients that can be quickly assembled into good food. There are vegan ready-to-eat frozen entrées, side dishes, and desserts available, as well. If you find some that you like, have them on hand for hunger-emergencies.

Items such as frozen or fresh veggie burgers, soy crumbles, and smoked seitan and tempeh make a good basis for entrées. Try various brands and varieties to see which you like the best. Fake meats, tofu dogs, breakfast strips, and veggie burgers are also products to check out and have on hand if you know you'll use them. Chiliburgers or dogs, tofu and breakfast strip scramble, grilled burgers, seitan or tempeh "steaks," and TLT (tempeh or fake meat, lettuce, and tomato) club sandwiches can all be quickly assembled with these products.

You should have a well-stocked general market with a good produce department on your shopping route. Scope out the markets that stock a fair amount of the ingredients you like to eat, such as soymilk, rice milk, soy cheese, nondairy ice cream and sorbets, tofu, whole wheat flour, etc. If not, either get friendly with the store manager or check out new markets. It's no fun to have to make three or four stops to acquire all your ingredients.

Stocking the Shelves

In the food service industry, we talk about par stocks. Pars are the amounts of products you use on a regular basis and you want to keep them level at all times. For example, you probably know when you're down to half a can of coffee or four slices of bread it's time to replenish. Keeping a mental or written par stock of ingredients is a good way to ensure that you'll always be able to put together a good meal. As part of your par, keep a supply of storage containers on hand, for refrigerating and freezing food and for transporting food to work or school. If you save containers from food products, be sure to check the label to be sure that

18

they are reusable. For example, some microwave containers state that they are single use containers.

Remember that there are some things that will last forever, and some things that become alien life forms after three days. And, although the freezer is a good storage area, it's not meant to keep items until the next Ice Age. In Chapter 2 we'll talk more about specific ingredients to have on hand.

A Place for Everything and Everything in its Place (or Wash Your Hands and Keep it Clean)

Professional chefs organize their work according to the principles of *mise en place*. Loosely translated, it means "everything it its place." What it means in practice is to pretend your meal prep-arations are occurring in front of a TV camera (Julia Child does Vegan!). Imagine that, once started, you can't go "off camera" or move from your spot (unless you have to walk to the stove). Add "clean as you go," and you're cooking like the professionals.

This means weigh, measure, open cans, chop, dice and slice, put pans on the stove and mixing bowls on the counter, and do whatever needs to be done to ensure the smooth preparation of your meal. This may sound like a lot of work and organization; however after you've done it several times, you'll see how easy it makes kitchen life!

Which leads us into the next topic. We're sure you've seen the bumper sticker "your mother doesn't work here, so clean up after yourself!" Unfortunately, the same goes when you're in your own kitchen. Practice the policy of *mise en place* when it comes to clean-up, too.

Be sure that your refrigerator and freezer are working well. Invest in a thermometer and check that your refrigerator is at or below 40 degrees (38 degrees is better) and that your freezer is at zero degrees. Be sure that you've arranged the items in the refrigerator and freezer so that air can circulate around the shelves. That's the way you get chilling. If your refrigerator and freezer are really tightly packed, then air can't move around and cool air can't get to all the products.

Even though there's lots of publicity about people getting food-borne illnesses in restaurants, there are actually more cases of homemade food-borne illness than public cases. Being vegan helps a bit, as there are no animal products to contaminate food. However, all protein-containing food will support bacterial growth. Cooked beans, soy products, rice, pasta, and raw or cooked vegetables or fruit can all be hosts to E. coli, staph, listeria, campylobacter, and salmonella bacteria. Doesn't this sound gruesome?

Bacteria that cause food-borne illness are easily contained. Use anti-bacterial soap or a rinse of diluted bleach on anything that touches food (this includes your hands!). Cutting boards, tables, dishes, glasses and cups, eating and cooking utensils, dish racks, sponges, etc. all need to be sanitized with chemicals (like bleach) or with heat (like a dishwasher that reaches at least 180 degrees). This will prevent bacterial growth. No more rinsing your coffee spoon under lukewarm water and storing it on the dish rack to be used to stir the soup later in the day.

Keep hot foods hot and cold foods cold. Refrigerate or freeze leftover portions of food, milk, mayonnaise, juice, and cut fruit until you're ready to eat them. Really reheat leftovers. Don't just tickle them! If you follow these guidelines, the only thing you'll have to worry about with your food is if you'll like the new recipe, not if bacteria is lurking in it!

Preparing Meals for One or Two

In this fast-moving day and age, it doesn't matter if you are a family of one or ten. You'll be preparing small meals at one time or another. Everybody's schedule is different and everyone seems to have different food preferences. With this book, there are no more excuses for choosing the fast food option. You can eat healthy and vegan. You'll feel mentally and physically pampered, as you will be giving your body what it needs. At the same time, you'll be nourishing your soul, as you sit down to personally-tailored, health-giving meals.

When we wrote this book, we meant for it to provide the information needed to prepare fun, comforting, exciting, semi-easy, semi-quick meals. Yes, everyone eats out from time to time and everyone microwaves a frozen meal. But it's a good feeling to have a repertoire of meals that you love and can easily prepare. Everyone desires to enjoy their meals, but nobody wants to spend their life in a kitchen or have to eat the same meal for a week.

We hope this book fulfills the desire for smaller quantity vegan meals that are a pleasure to eat. So put some flowers on the table, get out the good silver or your favorite mug, start cooking, and have fun!

Chapter Two

Meal Planning and Shopping

There are many ways to plan for a balanced diet, vegan or not. The key is variety. Variety should come easily, as very few people are happy with a monotonous diet (we know, except some two-year-olds that choose to live mainly on peanut butter sandwiches for months at a time). Does this mean that you need to have a thousand different ingredients in your kitchen? No. It does mean, that in addition to bread, pasta, crackers, and cake (which are all usually wheat-based), have some potatoes and rice for your starch quota. If you're buying canned or frozen veggies, buy something other than peas. If cold cereal is a main-stay, read labels – one may have more B vitamins and one may have more iron – and select several different kinds, so that you get a variety of nutrients. Store your cereals in airtight containers or food bags so they don't go stale. Whether hot or cold cereal is your meal, charge it up with fresh, frozen, or dried fruit, chopped nuts, wheat germ, or nutritional yeast. Do you get the variety picture?

We've included a guideline that hits the highlights of vegan meal planning, and a sample menu to give you an idea of how to apply it. Within each group, be sure to pick the foods that you enjoy and will eat. You can't absorb any nutrients from the two pounds of kale slowly growing roots in your refrigerator.

Vegan Meal Planning

The following information is adapted from *Meatless Meals for Working People,* by Debra Wasserman and Charles Stahler, 2001. This information is for adults who are not pregnant or breast-feeding. Teens, athletes, and pregnant and breast-feeding women may need additional servings.

1. High Protein Foods (1-2 servings/day)

8 ounces tofu
1-1/2 cups cooked beans or legumes
4 ounces tempeh
2 cups fortified soymilk
1/2 cup nuts
1/4 cup peanuts
4 Tablespoons peanut or soy butter
4-8 ounces fake meats or meat analogs

2. Grains and Whole Grains (6-10 servings per day)

1 slice whole-grain, whole-wheat, or rye bread
1 whole-wheat waffle or pancake
One 2-inch by 2-inch serving of cornbread
2 Tablespoons wheat germ, wheat bran, or oat bran
1/4 cup sunflower, sesame, or pumpkin seeds
3/4 cup whole-grain cereal, such as bran flakes or whole-wheat Cheerios
1/2 cup whole-grain cooked cereal, such as oatmeal
1/2 cup cooked grains, such as brown rice, barley, bulgur, amaranth, quinoa, or kasha
1/2 cup cooked whole-grain or vegetable pasta

3. Veggies (4-6 servings per day)

A. At least two of the following per day (1/2 cup cooked or 1 cup raw): broccoli, broccoflower, brocollini (a cross between chard and Chinese broccoli), Chinese flowering broccoli, broccoli rabe, Brussels sprouts, green cabbage, Napa cabbage, endive, chicory, kale, Swiss chard, mustard, collard or beet greens, spinach, Romaine lettuce, carrots, sweet potatoes, winter squash (such as butternut or spaghetti squash), tomatoes, or bell peppers

B. Two or more servings of any other veggies

4. Fruit (4-6 servings per day)

A. At least two servings of the following per day: cantaloupe or other orange-fleshed melons, watermelon, mango, papaya, orange, grapefruit, tangerine, peach, apricot, kiwi, strawberries, or vitamin C-enriched juices

B. At least two more servings of fresh, dried, or canned (in water or juice) fruit

Be sure to include good sources of calcium (at least 2 servings per day) which include fortified soy products, almonds, sesame seeds, and greens. Also include sources of vitamin B12, such as some fortified cereals and soymilks, Vegetarian Support Formula nutritional yeast, and some fortified fake meats.

Sample Menu

Breakfast

✓ Orange juice or Pink grapefruit sections (pink grapefruit have more of some vitamins than white grapefruit!)

✓ Toaster waffle with peanut butter and fruit preserves or Raisin bran with soymilk

✓ Sliced banana or Cantaloupe chunks

Lunch

✓ Lentil soup or Hummus and crackers

✓ Pita sandwich with grilled veggies or Pasta salad with veggies and olives

✓ Carrot salad with vegan mayonnaise or Baked sweet potato with margarine

✓ Fresh pear or apple

Dinner

✓ Tomato juice with a celery stalk or Sliced kiwi and strawberries

✓ Baked vegetable lasagna or Baked eggplant and mushrooms

✓ Dinner roll or bread sticks with margarine

✓ Tossed green salad with vinaigrette or Carrot sticks and radishes

✓ Apple cobbler or Soy ice cream with dried fruit

Snacks

✓ Graham crackers with peanut butter or hazelnut butter and fortified soymilk

✓ Popcorn sprinkled with Red Star nutritional yeast and orange-cranberry juice

✓ Soymilk, banana, and fruit smoothie

✓ Toasted bagel with fruit preserves or apple butter

Shopping and Stocking

When we cook, we like to keep it as simple as possible. So look at your budget and your food philosophy and see if the following ideas fit into your kitchen schemes:

1. If ingredients come pre-chopped, sliced, diced, or pre-cooked, think about using them. Not all the time, and not for everything, but convenience ingredients may make the difference between you preparing a decent meal for yourself and opting out for yet another bowl of dried cereal.

2. Keep a good selection of canned beans and canned vegetables. It would be wonderful if we all had the time and inclination to shop for and prepare fresh vegetables and dried beans. The reality of life, however, is that it doesn't always happen. So be prepared. If you have the ingredients at hand, you'll prepare the meal. We have seen canned lentils, kidney, black, white, lima, butter (baby limas), garbanzo, and soybeans, to name a few. Yes, we know that fresh or frozen veggies are generally higher in nutrients and lower in sodium than canned veggies, but canned veggies are better than no veggies, and are good add-in ingredients. We like to keep canned corn, green

beans, wax beans, sliced or julienne beets, sliced carrots, sauerkraut, pickled red cabbage, sliced or whole mushrooms, chopped tomatoes, whole potatoes, mustard greens, collard greens, and mushrooms on hand.

3.   Both dried fruit and veggies are good. Dried dates, apricots, figs, raisins, prunes, apples, peaches, nectarines, cranberries, cherries, and blueberries are just some of the dried fruit that you can toss into cereal, pancakes, smoothies, and green or fruit salads, or just eat them out-of-hand. Dried fruit is high in (natural) sugar, but as snacks and ingredients go, they are chock-full of nutrients. Sun-dried red and yellow tomatoes, dried veggie soup mixes, dried mushrooms, and dried chilies are easy additions to soups, salads, pastas, and combination dishes.

4.   Think ethnic. Just picture it – you unceremoniously dump a can of white beans into a bowl. Big deal. Now you toss in some salsa. Hmmm, getting better. For you fire-eaters out there, add some pickled jalapeños and hot sauce. Throw your feast into the microwave until it's hot and you've got something spectacular! Prowl Indian stores for curry pastes and powders, aromatic sauce mixes, tandoori rubs (great for vegetables and tofu), pickled veggies, rice, chutneys, long-grained rice, and interesting breads and cracker breads. Visit Middle Eastern stores for spices, hummus, tahini, harira (a fiery chili paste), pomegranate molasses (makes a wonderful addition to salad dressings and cold beverages), nut and seed blends, and breads. Asian markets yield different varieties of tofu, soy beverages, spices, sauces, great canned fruits and vegetables, long- and short-grained rice, and different varieties of produce.

5.   Pasta and rice are available fresh and frozen, plain and prepared. Decide what you like and what you'll have time to prepare. A quick tip: fresh pasta sold in the refrigerated section of the market can be frozen. So you don't have to eat that entire package of angel hair pasta. Cook what

you'll eat and freeze the rest (remember to read the label to make sure the fresh pasta does not contain eggs!). Pasta and rice come in other colors besides white. Think brown, wild, and even black rice. Pasta can be spinach, carrot, tomato, mushroom, chili, and lemon-basil, to name a few.

6. Consider pre-cut or bagged salad, vegetables, or fruit. Yes, they can be more expensive than uncut produce. But it seems better to spend a little more for a container of cut cantaloupe chunks rather than saying, "I love cantaloupe, but I'll never eat the whole thing." The same goes for salad. Just Romaine or spinach in the bowl is okay, but to avoid salad-burnout, the bagged salads offer interesting combinations. We like to buy the pre-cut coleslaw mix (usually shredded green cabbage and carrots) or bagged, shredded red cabbage, then sauté either one with a little bit of oil and a lot of cracked pepper. Mix the cabbage with cooked broad noodles and you have a fast supper.

7. While watching the fat in your diet, oil is still an important ingredient, adding both flavor and color. Olive oil is flavorful and high in monounsaturated fat (one of the good guys). Sesame seed and hazelnut oils are specialty oils that give unique flavors to dishes. If you're selecting just plain vegetable oil, read the label to find the most unsaturated kind. Vegetable oil sprays are very useful for cooking (you'll see a lot of that in the recipes in this book, rather than liquid oil). Margarine is not necessarily vegan (or unsaturated), so read the labels for the healthiest type. Some health experts advise limiting the amount of trans-fatty acids in the diet. These can be found in solid margarine and products such as cookies or snack bars made with solid margarine or hydrogenated oils. Again, read the label. You'll want to really limit products that contain palm and coconut oils, as they are high in saturated fats. Remember that 1-1/4 teaspoons of most oils contain about 50 calories, all from fat. (Just thought we'd mention, for perspective, that about 4 ounces of fruit

juice contains about 60 calories and no fat, and a half-cup of most cooked veggies is 25 calories with no fat.)

8. Nuts, seeds, and nut butters add flavor and interest to your meals. Oatmeal can get exciting with some walnut or pecan crunch, and soups shine when garnished with toasted almonds or sesame seeds. We've seen soy, hazelnut, and almond butters on the market shelf. They are good! High in fat, yes, but used sparingly they can add a lot of flavor, color, and crunch to your menu.

9. Mix and match. For example – consider canned tomato soup. Yawn. But add some canned tomatoes... chunked tofu... canned garbanzo beans... and some leftover baked potato. It is absolutely legal to mix and match your ingredients. Add nuts and dried fruit to pancake and waffle mixes; frozen and fresh berries to muffin mixes; canned mushrooms and dried chilies to cup-of-noodles; or granola and nuts to instant pudding.

10. Think ethnic, revisited. When you go to a restaurant in an ethnic area, check out the neighborhood groceries. You'll probably find some vegan convenience ingredients that will spice up your meals. Indulge in frozen entrées and side dishes, or soup, sauce, or dessert mixes. Indian dahl (lentil soup, used as a universal condiment), Mexican tamales (many places are making them with vegetable oil instead of lard; just ask), Persian pita, Israeli falafel, Thai mango and sticky rice, and Russian beet borscht are just some of the prepared items we like to bring home. You can base a wonderful meal around any of these.

11. Spice rack: always have the sweet staples (cinnamon, nutmeg, orange zest, ground ginger, cloves, etc.) and the savory (granulated garlic, black and white pepper, onion powder, dried basil, oregano, thyme, red pepper flakes, curry powder, dried parsley, etc.). Add spice blends, such as lemon-pepper or Cajun spices, if you know you'll use them. Do discard dried herbs and spice that have lost their

zing. Even if stored in a cool, dry place in an airtight container, most dried herbs and spices lose their flavoring capacity after a year.

12. Look in the refrigerator: depending upon your preferences, have a nice stock of firm and silken tofu, tempeh, and/or seitan. Purchase them plain or flavored, as you like them. Fake meats, such as deli slices, veggie hot dogs, and breakfast crumbles freeze well and are great add-in ingredients. Tofu, tempeh, and seitan also freeze well. For example, if you move a package of tofu and a package of soy crumbles (see the glossary) from the freezer to the refrigerator in the morning, they'll be thawed by the time you are ready to make dinner. Sauté the crumbles (in oil, margarine, or vegetable oil spray) with some chopped veggies, scramble in the tofu, and top with salsa or tomato sauce, and you have a fast, hot meal.

13. Say cheese: vegan soy cheese that is. There are lots of vegan cheese and "dairy" products on the market today, such as flavored, shredded, and sliced soy cheese; soy sour cream and cream cheese; and soy yogurt. Experiment with different brands and products until you find the ones you like. Most soy cheese can be frozen.

14. Bread and crackers are even faster to use than pasta or rice, and some freeze very well. You can make a fast "pizza" if you've got English muffins in the freezer and chopped tomatoes and tomato sauce in the pantry. Quick burritos require tortillas. Make a stuffed sandwich using pita.

15. Rooting for the veggies: root vegetables can be stored for a long time, so select your favorites from white potatoes, purple potatoes (called Peruvian purples, they are dark purple on the outside and lavender on the inside), Yukon golds, sweet potatoes, carrots, onions, garlic, beets, and turnips. Give them a dark, cool home and toss them into the oven to bake, or steam them on top of the stove or in

the microwave. Top a white baked potato with canned lentils and salsa, or top a sweet potato with crushed pine-apple, mashed tofu, dried cranberries, and canned mandarin oranges. Root veggies can be mashed with margarine or vegetable stock and eaten as a side dish, or puréed and used as the basis of soup. Need some snack food? Thinly slice fresh beets, purple potatoes, Yukon Gold potatoes, carrots, and taro (if you've got it). Place them on an oil-sprayed baking sheet and bake at 425 degrees until they are crispy, hot, fresh chips. Serve them with salsa, pizza sauce, or hummus and you've got a great (and inexpensive) snack.

We realize this sounds like a lot of food to have on hand, and it is. You need to select the items you like and will use. Remember, you have to decide on the balance between too few, boring staples and over-the-top stocking. Make your kitchen a friendly, welcoming place. Know that, when you are thinking about what to have for breakfast, what to pack for lunch, or what to make for dinner, there are lots of ingredients you enjoy and can combine to make healthy, pleasing meals. Your time in the kitchen, and your meal times, should be pleasant, encouraging times. It's all up to you!

Tools of the Trade

Just as you need to select the ingredients you know you will use, select kitchen equipment with which you're comfortable. The recipes in this book require a minimum amount of equipment, while still taking advantage of labor-saving devices.

Tools including a good knife (and a way to sharpen it) and a cutting board; several mixing bowls; a small and a large frying pan; a small and a large pot (with lids); several baking dishes; a blender and a microwave; along with the usual necessities such as a can opener, stirring spoons, spatulas, and a strainer or colander should do it. We're assuming you remember where the stovetop and the oven are, and that they are in good shape (i.e., the stove burners stay lit and the oven actually heats to the temperature at which you set it). Be sure to have a good supply of foil and plastic wrap on hand, as well as an assortment of storage containers for extra portions of foods and ingredients.

If you like kitchen gadgets, you can certainly find a use for a food processor, an electric mixer, an electric can opener, a spice grinder, a coffee (or tea) brewer, a dehydrator, and a barbecue grill. These are not necessary for the recipes in this book. A microwave is not necessary, just a time saver. We've included directions for conventional and microwave cooking. If you are using a microwave, be sure you have an assortment of micro-wave-safe dishes along with lids.

Kitchen Safety

Keep lots of towels, soap, and bleach or bleach alternatives around. If you use sponges and towels, sanitize them frequently with diluted bleach or in the dishwasher. Bacteria are rendered harmless by water that is over 180 degrees or by chlorine, so make your choice (you don't need both, just one or the other).

Avoid cross-contamination (spreading bacteria from a utensil or food to another utensil or food) by sanitizing your hands and utensils every time you switch dishes. You don't have to peel fruit and veggies if you don't want to, but you do have to wash and scrub them well.

Label and date prepared food and ingredients. Do a refrig-erator-sweep at least every five days. Discard what no longer resembles its label description. If you think you won't eat some-thing in a day or two, freeze it. Remember to thaw foods in the refrigerator, not on the counter. (Unless your kitchen is below 40 degrees or above 140 degrees.) Invest in a thermometer to check the refrigerator, the freezer, and the oven. This will not only ensure that you keep foods safe, but will keep them fresher. In the case of the oven, foods will be cooked properly and evenly. If you have a dishwasher, you might want to check it with the thermometer to be sure it's getting up to a sanitizing temperature. Remember that everything can be cleaned and sanitized. That means the oven racks, the inside of the freezer, the interior of the dishwasher, and the pantry shelves. We won't mention your travel cup and your insulated lunch bag.

Store foods safely. In the pantry, everything should be off the floor, in airtight containers, and there should be enough room between boxes, cans, and containers so that air can circulate. The same goes for the refrigerator and the freezer. If air can't get around, then the cool air can't get around either. If anything is going to drip in the refrigerator (like a package of thawing tofu), then place it on the bottom shelf, so it can't drip onto foods beneath it.

Don't get too attached to pots, pans, and utensils. If they rust, scratch, chip, corrode, crack, or discolor, it's time to say "bye-bye." Remember, when the coating starts disappearing from your nonstick pan, it's disappearing into your food (not a pleasant thought). And the scratches left in the remaining coating are a perfect place for bacteria to grow (another unpleasant thought). Try to avoid heavily painted serving dishes or eating dishes, especially for storing food. You don't want paint chips or heavy metals, such as lead or mercury (sometimes used in paint pigments) in your food.

This probably sounds like a lot of information. But don't fret, we don't expect you to become health inspectors. Once you've set up your safe kitchen and have a routine, you won't remember doing it any other way.

Okay, you're stocked, stoked, and ready to go – let's cook!

Chapter Three

Breakfast

Breakfast is the most important meal of the day, and probably the most neglected. Until someone figures out how to get room service to our bedrooms, work, or school, morning breakfasts will most likely be of the grab-and-go variety. With a bit of planning, you can have a hot breakfast several mornings a week and a hearty cold breakfast the rest of the week.

Are you not hungry when you get up or not willing to alter your 12.5 minute from-the-alarm-to-out-the-door routine? Then pack a breakfast the night before and eat it at the bus stop or when you get to the office. We do not advocate eating while driving (talking on the cell phone and applying make-up is bad enough).

We understand that the a.m. meal may be simply cereal and soymilk. Okay. But always go for the value-added (in this case, the value is "nutrition"). Toss some dried fruit and/or nuts into your cereal. Try to have some fresh seasonal fruit hanging around to slice into the cereal. You can even mix several kinds of cold cereal together to complement the nutritional value of each one and to create new flavors. If you have no time for even cereal, make up small bags of cereal and purchase individual soy or rice milks; add a banana or an orange (or both), and you have a perfect briefcase breakfast. This chapter includes several different granola recipes. Select the one you like, prepare it ahead of time, and toss it in with your cereal or bring separate bags.

Tofu is very workable for breakfast. There is a recipe for a tofu scramble later in this chapter. With coordination, you should be able to do this recipe easily in 5-7 minutes. Tofu can be scrambled with onions, peppers, and hot sauce or (for a really quick scramble) just salsa for savory breakfasts. Or you can go with bananas, nuts, berries, and orange juice concentrate added

34

to the tofu for a sweet breakfast. If you don't have time to scramble, mix tofu in a baking dish and allow it to bake, as a breakfast casserole, while you're getting ready to leave. Check out the almond-flavored and sweetened prepared tofu available in Asian markets. You can spoon this right out of the container for a needs-no-preparation breakfast.

The freezer can be your friend for fast (and slow) breakfasts. Purchase frozen berries when fresh ones are not in season (or if you know that you won't eat the fresh ones before they start growing fur). Thaw a handful of berries in a covered container and use them on hot or cold cereal, mashed on English muffins or toast (berries are especially good smashed into nut butters), or blended into smoothies. When you have time to cook, include fresh berries in pancakes, waffles, and muffins.

No time to chew? The blender is the answer. Build a meal-in-a-cup the night before. Load the blender or food processor canister with fresh or frozen fruit, tofu or soy yogurt, apple sauce, Red Star nutritional yeast, fruit juice, etc. You get the picture. Combine everything in the blender canister and leave it in the refrigerator over night. Just blend away in the morning. Leftover smoothie can be taken to work in an insulated cup or thermos or frozen as your own personal frozen dessert for later in the day.

Don't forget to plan! Here are some items to have on hand (yes, we know this is a lot of food; select what you know you'll eat):

Freezer
- frozen berries, such as strawberries, blueberries, and raspberries
- frozen waffle or pancake batter
- frozen fruit, such as peach slices and melon balls
- soy or rice milk ice cream (hey, everybody needs an a.m. change of pace!)
- frozen burritos (see note on ice cream)
- frozen pizza (ditto)
- frozen muffins and bagels

Refrigerator
- plain or flavored soy or rice milk
- fruit and/or vegetable juice
- soy yogurt
- plain or flavored tofu (look for almond-flavored tofu in Asian markets; it's a breakfast by itself)
- English muffins, sliced bread
- fresh fruit and fruit preserves
- vegan margarine
- Red Star Vegetarian Formula (nutritional yeast)

Pantry
- assorted coffee, tea, and hot cocoa mixes
- vegetable oil spray
- spice rack: dry sweetener, cinnamon, nutmeg, ginger, mace, dried orange and lemon zest, ground cloves, etc.
- assorted cold cereal
- assorted hot cereal (instant or long-cooking; your call)
- instant cup-of-cereal products
- dried fruit, such as raisins, apricots, cranberries, prunes, apples, etc.
- trail mix or granola
- graham crackers
- nuts, such as walnuts, almonds, pecans, Brazil nuts, etc., and hulled seeds, such as sunflower or pumpkin
- shredded coconut
- nut butters (peanut, almond, hazelnut, soy, etc.)
- canned beans
- canned fruit, including applesauce
- prepared salsa
- individual soy or rice milks
- individual juices (preferably containing vitamin C)

Equipment (just suggestions, not mandatory)
- microwave (very important for fast morning eat-and-goes)
- coffee or tea maker
- toaster oven
- blender or food processor
- assorted pots and pan
- lots of storage containers and bags

Here are some fast ideas to get you started:

❖ Cold cereal with fresh or thawed frozen fruit and dried fruit, with soy, rice, or grain milk

❖ Trail mix with soymilk and a banana, mango (look for frozen mango cubes, they have a great flavor), or melon cubes

❖ Microwave a frozen blueberry or zucchini muffin and eat with peanut butter and fruit preserves

❖ Create fruit smoothies

❖ Breakfast "pizza" – a toasted English muffin or bagel piled high with peanut butter, chopped nuts, chopped dried fruit, and fruit preserves

❖ Microwave a frozen burrito; eat with a cup of juice or some fruit

❖ Breakfast "sundae" – frozen soy or rice milk ice cream with fresh or thawed frozen fruit, chopped nuts, Red Star nutritional yeast, and sliced bananas

❖ Microwave instant hot cereal, slice some fruit or sprinkle some berries on top, and add nutritional yeast and nuts

❖ Use instant "cup of cereals" as a base for a fast but hot breakfast. Toss in chopped dried fruit, granola, fresh or thawed frozen berries, sliced fresh or canned peaches, pears, apricots, sliced bananas, chopped nuts, nutritional yeast, and a sprinkle of cinnamon, nutmeg, or ginger

❖ Even instant couscous can be a good breakfast, with the addition of chopped dried fruit and nuts

Recipes

The following breakfast recipes are for the days when you have more time for preparation the night before. Pancakes and French toast can be prepared ahead of time and reheated the next morning while you are getting ready to go, or reheated at work or school. Extra portions can be eaten as dessert with sorbet, sliced fresh fruit and berries, or just reheated with fruit preserves.

Most of these recipes will probably take a little more time than you might have on workday mornings. Make one or two of them on your days off and refrigerate or freeze the extra portions (if there are any!) to reheat during the work week. Many of the following recipes make great entertaining dishes for brunches or even for desserts.

Tofu Scramble
(Makes 1 hearty serving)

This is an easy recipe, made to your preference!

1 cup plain firm tofu, drained and crumbled
Vegetable oil spray
1/4 cup chopped leftover veggies
2 Tablespoons salsa

In a small bowl, mash tofu. Heat a small frying pan and spray with oil. Place tofu in the pan and mix in veggies. Stir and sauté until the veggies are soft and the tofu is heated through. Mix in the salsa and allow scramble to cook until heated.

Serve hot on it's own, wrapped in a tortilla or pita, or with cooked potatoes or rice.

Total Calories Per Serving Using Chopped Green Peppers and Onions: 395
Total Fat as % of Daily Value: 35%
Protein: 41 gm   Fat: 23 gm   Carbohydrates: 15 gm   Calcium: 429 mg
Iron: 27 mg   Sodium: 120 mg   Dietary Fiber: 7 gm

Corny French Toast
(Makes 3 slices)

Add some crunch to your French toast; you can get your cereal, bread, and milk all in one dish.

2 Tablespoons silken tofu
1/4 cup vanilla soy or rice milk
1/4 teaspoon nutmeg
1/2 teaspoon cinnamon
1 cup cornflakes
3 slices whole wheat or raisin bread
Vegetable oil spray

In a bowl, combine tofu, milk, nutmeg, and cinnamon until smooth.

Crumble cornflakes (you're not looking for cornflake flour; crumble until each flake is broken in two or three pieces). Spread flakes on a dinner plate.

Dip bread in the tofu mixture until both sides are coated. Place each slice of bread (both sides) into the cornflakes. Press down slightly so they stick. Spray frying pan with vegetable oil and fry bread until each side is golden brown.

Serve with sliced bananas, fruit preserves, or syrup.

Notes: If you don't have vanilla flavored soy or rice milk, use plain and add a half-teaspoon of vanilla extract and a quarter teaspoon sweetener. If you're not into frying (or you want to have breakfast cooking while you do other things), you can bake this recipe. Preheat oven to 375 degrees while you prepare the bread. Spray a baking sheet with vegetable oil and place the prepared bread on it. Bake for approximately 20 minutes or until golden and puffy.

Total Calories Per Serving Using Soymilk and Whole Wheat Bread: 385
Total Fat as % of Daily Value: 11%
Protein: 13 gm   Fat: 7 gm   Carbohydrates: 69 gm   Calcium: 107 mg
Iron: 4 mg   Sodium: 716 mg   Dietary Fiber: 7 gm

Cinnamon, Apple, and Raisin Pancakes

(Makes about 4 six-inch pancakes)

This Autumn-influenced recipe can be enjoyed throughout the year. In the cold months, eat with syrup and sliced apples and in the warm months serve with fresh berries.

1-1/2 cups all-purpose flour
1/4 cup vegan dry sweetener (see glossary)
2 teaspoons baking powder
2 teaspoons cinnamon
1 cup plain or vanilla soymilk
2 Tablespoons silken tofu
1 Tablespoon oil or melted margarine
1/4 teaspoon vanilla extract
Vegetable oil spray
2 large green apples (about 1 cup), peeled, cored, and
**   minced**
1/2 cup raisins

Sift flour, sweetener, baking powder, and cinnamon together and place in a large bowl. In a separate bowl, mix soymilk, tofu, oil or margarine, and vanilla together until well combined. Slowly mix dry and liquid ingredients together until smooth. Cover and refrigerate for at least 1 hour.

Heat a large frying pan and spray with oil. Add apples and raisins and sauté for 3 minutes or until apples begin to soften. Place in a bowl and set aside.

Respray pan and ladle batter into the pan by 1/2 cup measures. Top each with 2 Tablespoons of apple/raisin mixture. Cook until pancakes begin to bubble. Flip and cook until golden brown. Serve with maple syrup and additional raisins, if desired.

Note: This batter can be prepared the night before and left in the refrigerator overnight. For a faster version of this recipe, simply add apples and raisins to your favorite pancake mix.

Total Calories Per Pancake Using Plain Soymilk: 393
Total Fat as % of Daily Value: 9%
Protein: 8 gm   Fat: 6 gm   Carbohydrates: 76 gm   Calcium: 175 mg
Iron: 4 mg   Sodium: 256 mg   Dietary Fiber: 5 gm

Cinnamon and Potato Pancakes
(Makes 4 pancakes)

This is a great way to use up extra potatoes and a terrific way to put a new spin on pancakes!

Vegetable oil spray
2 cups frozen hash brown potatoes, thawed (or cooked, leftover hash browns)
2 teaspoons cinnamon
2 cups prepared pancake batter

Spray a large frying pan with oil. Add hash browns and cook until crisp. Sprinkle with cinnamon. Divide potatoes into six separate stacks in the pan and pour 1/2 cup pancake batter onto each stack. Mix each stack with the batter, right in the pan. Cook until each side is golden brown. Serve with syrup and sliced bananas, if desired.

Note: The potatoes can be cooked the night before and reheated the next day. If you have a leftover baked potato, you can slice it and use it for hash browns.

Total Calories Per Pancake Using Apple/Raisin Pancake Batter On Previous Page (minus apples and raisins): 450   Total Fat as % of Daily Value: 23%
Protein: 10 gm   Fat: 15 gm   Carbohydrates: 73 gm   Calcium: 173 mg
Iron: 4 mg   Sodium: 279 mg   Dietary Fiber: 4 gm

Macadamia Nut Pancakes
(Makes 4 pancakes)

This recipe is definitely a "special day" recipe. Please note the batter needs to stand for at least an hour before being cooked (you can prepare it the night before and store it in the refrigerator). If macadamias are not available, you can substitute chopped walnuts or pecans.

1/4 cup flour
1/4 teaspoon dry sweetener
1/4 teaspoon baking powder
1/8 teaspoon baking soda
1 Tablespoon firm tofu
1/4 cup vanilla soy, rice, or nut milk
Vegetable oil spray
1/4 cup unsalted toasted macadamia nuts, chopped
1/2 cup canned crushed pineapple (optional topping)

Sift flour, sweetener, baking powder, and baking soda into a small bowl. In a separate bowl beat tofu and milk together until very foamy. Pour liquid ingredients into dry ingredients and stir only to combine (do not over mix). Let stand 1 hour.

Heat a large frying pan and spray with oil. Spoon batter in 2 Tablespoon amounts into the pan and sprinkle with nuts. Cook until tops are bubbly, flip, and cook until the second side is golden.

Serve while hot with the pineapple that you have heated.

Note: This will work with other chopped nuts, if macadamias are too much for the budget or the fat inventory.

Total Calories Per Pancake Using Vanilla Soymilk: 121
Total Fat as % of Daily Value: 11%
Protein: 2 gm   Fat: 7 gm   Carbohydrates: 13 gm   Calcium: 39 mg
Iron: 1 mg   Sodium: 79 mg   Dietary Fiber: 1 gm

Breakfast Potato Burritos

(Makes 3 burritos)

This recipe will do for lunch and supper, too!

Vegetable oil spray
1 cup frozen hash browns, thawed
1/2 cup cooked soy crumbles (see glossary)
1/4 cup chopped bell pepper
1/4 cup chopped green onions
1 chopped chili (if desired)
4 Tablespoons firm tofu, crumbled
3 ten-inch flour tortillas

Spray a large frying pan with oil. Brown potatoes. Add crumbles, pepper, onions, and chili and sauté until vegetables are soft, approximately 3 minutes. Add tofu and cook, tossing until well combined and heated through. Divide mixture into thirds and fill tortillas.

Note: Sliced mushrooms can be used instead of soy crumbles. These burritos can be assembled the night before and then heated in a 350 degree oven for 10 minutes the next day. The burritos can also be frozen.

Total Calories Per Burrito: 412   Total Fat as % of Daily Value: 23%
Protein: 13 gm   Fat: 15 gm   Carbohydrates: 59 gm   Calcium: 147 mg
Iron: 6 mg   Sodium: 482 mg   Dietary Fiber: 5 gm

Upside-Down Pecan-Bran Muffins

(Makes 8 large muffins)

You'll need time to bake for this recipe. However, the muffins are moist and will last up to a week in the refrigerator (or you can freeze the baked muffins).

Vegetable oil spray
1/3 cup vegan margarine
1/3 cup maple syrup
8 shelled and halved pecans (16 halves)
1 cup bran or smashed bran flakes
1/2 cup shelled and chopped pecans
1/2 cup flour (white or whole wheat are both fine)
2 Tablespoons dry sweetener
1 teaspoon orange zest
1 teaspoon baking soda
1/2 cup soy or rice milk
2 teaspoons lemon juice
6 Tablespoons maple syrup
1/4 cup melted vegan margarine
1/8 cup firm tofu

Preheat oven to 400 degrees. Spray 8 large muffin cups (should hold 1/4 cup each) with vegetable oil. In a small pan, melt 1/3 cup margarine. Mix in 1/3 cup maple syrup. Pour mixture into the bottom of the muffin cups. Put 2 pecan halves in the bottom of each cup. Set aside.

In a large bowl, mix bran, chopped pecans, flour, sweetener, orange zest, and baking soda together. In a separate bowl, whisk together milk, juice, 6 Tablespoons maple syrup, 1/4 cup melted margarine, and tofu until well combined. Combine dry and moist ingredients together and mix until just combined (don't overmix).

Pour batter into muffin cups. Bake for approximately 30 minutes at 400 degrees or until muffin tops are golden brown and a knife inserted in the center comes out clean. Allow muffins to cool before removing from pan.

Total Calories Per Muffin: 319   Total Fat as % of Daily Value: 33%
Protein: 4 gm   Fat: 21 gm   Carbohydrates: 33 gm   Calcium: 41 mg
Iron: 2 mg   Sodium: 317 mg   Dietary Fiber: 4 gm

Revved-Up Oatmeal
(Makes 1-1/2 cups)

This is almost like a power bar in a bowl!

1 cup cooked instant oatmeal
1 teaspoon dry sweetener (if desired)
1 Tablespoon raisins
1 Tablespoon wheat germ
1/2 cup soy or rice milk (use vanilla-flavored, if you like)

Combine all ingredients in a microwave-safe bowl and heat for 2 minutes on high or until thoroughly heated. Or combine all ingredients in a small pot and cook over medium heat, stirring for 5 minutes or until thoroughly heated. Eat while hot.

Total Calories Per Serving Using Soymilk: 240
Total Fat as % of Daily Value: 8%
Protein: 12 gm   Fat: 5 gm   Carbohydrates: 39 gm   Calcium: 32 mg
Iron: 3 mg   Sodium: 20 mg   Dietary Fiber: 7 gm

Apple Yogurt
(Makes 1-1/4 cups)

This yogurt can be eaten on its own, served over cold cereal, or even used for a dessert sauce over cake or cookies.

1 cup unflavored or berry-flavored soy yogurt
2 Tablespoons apple butter
1 Tablespoon unsweetened applesauce
1/2 teaspoon ground cinnamon

In a small bowl, combine all the ingredients. Eat right away or store in the refrigerator until ready to eat. Use as a topping for pancakes or instead of milk for cold cereal.

Total Calories Per Serving: 264   Total Fat as % of Daily Value: 17%
Protein: 13 gm   Fat: 11 gm   Carbohydrates: 30 gm   Calcium: 291 mg
Iron: 15 mg   Sodium: 19 mg   Dietary Fiber: 3 gm

Apple Oatmeal
(Makes 1-1/2 cups)

Add some crunch and sweetness to your morning oatmeal.

1 small apple, cored and chopped
1/2 cup apple juice
1 teaspoon cinnamon
2/3 cup rolled oats (oatmeal)
1/4 cup chopped walnuts

In a medium-sized pot, combine all the ingredients and bring to a fast boil. Reduce heat and simmer, stirring for 5 minutes or until oatmeal is cooked to the texture you like. Eat while hot.

Total Calories Per Serving: 516   Total Fat as % of Daily Value: 34%
Protein: 13 gm   Fat: 22 gm   Carbohydrates: 72 gm   Calcium: 99 mg
Iron: 4 mg   Sodium: 9 mg   Dietary Fiber: 11 gm

Your Own Granola
(Makes about 4 cups)

Munch on this throughout the day and throughout the week. Add granola to hot or cold cereal, or if you're baking, add it to muffin batter.

1/2 cup maple syrup
1/4 cup vegan margarine
2 cups rolled oats (long-cooking oatmeal)
1/4 cup shredded coconut
1/2 cup chopped pecans, Brazil nuts, cashews, or
    walnuts (or a mixture)
1/3 cup hulled pumpkin seeds or sunflower seeds

Preheat oven to 375 degrees. In a small pan, heat syrup and margarine; stir and cook until margarine is melted.

In a medium-sized baking dish combine oats, coconut, nuts, and seeds and pack down to form a consistent flat layer. Pour margarine and syrup mixture evenly over oat mixture.

Bake at 375 degrees for 25 minutes or until golden brown, stirring occasionally. The granola can be stored at room temperature in an airtight container.

Total Calories Per 1/2 Cup Serving: 269
Total Fat as % of Daily Value: 24%
Protein: 6 gm   Fat: 15 gm   Carbohydrates: 30 gm   Calcium: 34 mg
Iron: 2 mg   Sodium: 71 mg   Dietary Fiber: 3 gm

Ginger-Molasses Crunch
(Makes 4 servings)

Here's a different spin on granola. Use it as a cold cereal or moisten with milk and heat it in the microwave or on top of the stove for hot cereal. Makes a wonderful snack, too.

1-1/2 cups oat bran
1 cup oats (not instant)
1 Tablespoon margarine, melted
1/4 cup maple syrup
1 Tablespoon molasses (can be dark or light)
1 teaspoon lemon zest
1/2 teaspoon vanilla
1 teaspoon ground ginger
1/4 cup dried cranberries or raisins
Vegetable oil spray

Heat oven to 375 degrees. In a large bowl, mix oat bran and oats and set aside. In a medium bowl, combine remaining ingredients (except oil spray). Combine oats and other mixture.

Spray a cookie sheet with vegetable oil. Spread oat mixture in an even layer on the sheet. Bake at 375 degrees for 20 minutes, stirring twice, or until golden. Store in an airtight container.

Total Calories Per Serving: 283   Total Fat as % of Daily Value: 11%
Protein: 10 gm   Fat: 7 gm   Carbohydrates: 60 gm   Calcium: 58 mg
Iron: 3 mg   Sodium: 40 mg   Dietary Fiber: 8 gm

Fruit Granola
(Makes 5 cups)

This granola has more fruit than most granolas. Enjoy the added sweetness, texture, and nutrients.

2 cups rolled oats (not instant oatmeal)
3/4 cups cereal flakes (like bran or wheat flakes)
1/2 cup hulled sunflower seeds
1/2 cup chopped nuts (one type or combos – it's your choice)
1/4 cup oil
1/8 cup apple juice concentrate
1/4 cup raisins
1/4 cup chopped dried apricots or peaches
1/4 cup chopped dried apples
1/4 cup dried berries (such as cranberries, cherries or blueberries)

Preheat oven to 425 degrees. In a large bowl, combine oats, flakes, seeds, nuts, oil, and concentrate. Spread in the bottom of a large baking dish or roasting pan. Bake at 425 degrees until golden around the edges, stirring once or twice. This should take approximately 10-12 minutes.

Let cool completely. Stir in dried fruit. Store in an airtight container in a cool place, but not in the refrigerator (it will become soggy).

Total Calories Per 1/2 Cup Serving Using Wheat Flakes, Almonds and Walnuts, and Dried Apricots and Cranberries: 240
Total Fat as % of Daily Value: 20%
Protein: 6 gm   Fat: 13 gm   Carbohydrates: 26 gm   Calcium: 50 mg
Iron: 3 mg   Sodium: 26 mg   Dietary Fiber: 4 gm

Creamy Baked Fruit Gratin
(Makes 3 servings)

Using the previous Fruit Granola recipe, make this a soul-warming and good-reason-to-get-out-of-bed recipe. You can prepare it the night before and rewarm it in the oven as you're getting ready in the morning. (We have been known to use the extra portions as dessert, served with sorbet!)

2 cups Fruit Granola (see previous recipe)
1/2 cup soy, rice, or almond milk
1/4 cup silken tofu
1/8 cup dry sweetener
1 small sliced banana and 1/4 cup blueberries for garnish, if desired.

Preheat oven to 375 degrees. In a large bowl, mix all the ingredients together until well combined. Pour into a small baking dish and bake at 375 degrees until all the liquid is absorbed and top is golden, approximately 20 minutes.

Note: Don't tell anyone, but a scoop of soy or rice ice cream and a soy latte make a decadent snack or supper.

Total Calories Per Serving Using Soymilk: 408
Total Fat as % of Daily Value: 30%
Protein: 11 gm   Fat: 19 gm   Carbohydrates: 53 gm   Calcium: 77 mg
Iron: 5 mg   Sodium: 42 mg   Dietary Fiber: 6 gm

Hot Apples and Sweet Potatoes
(Makes 4 servings)

What a way to get your fruit in the morning! This makes a great hot breakfast and could also be a sweet side dish for spicy meals.

1/2 cup dry sweetener
1/2 teaspoon nutmeg
1/2 teaspoon cinnamon
1/2 teaspoon ground ginger
3/4 cup raw sweet potatoes, peeled and sliced very thin
1/8 cup canned crushed pineapple, drained
3/4 cup green apples, peeled, cored, and sliced very thin
1/2 cup granola (use any of the recipes in this chapter or commercial granola)
1/8 cup raisins, dried cranberries, or dried cherries
Vegetable oil spray

Preheat oven to 375 degrees. In a small bowl, mix sweetener, nutmeg, cinnamon, and ginger. In a medium-sized bowl, combine remaining ingredients except for oil spray. Combine spice and apple mixtures and mix well.

Spray a baking sheet with oil. Spread apple/sweet potato mixture on baking sheet and cover with foil. Bake at 375 degrees for 45 minutes or until potatoes and apples are soft. Eat while warm.

Total Calories Per Serving Using Raisins: 223
Total Fat as % of Daily Value: 4%
Protein: 2 gm   Fat: 3 gm   Carbohydrates: 50 gm   Calcium: 26 mg
Iron: 1 mg   Sodium: 28 mg   Dietary Fiber: 3 gm

Breakfast Snaps

(Makes about 10 snaps)

These are great for breakfast on-the-go.

1/2 cup shredded wheat, crushed
2 Tablespoons chopped pecans or walnuts
1 Tablespoon hulled pumpkin or sunflower seeds
1 cup cold cereal, crushed (flakes or crispies work well)
1/8 cup dry sweetener
2 teaspoons apple juice concentrate
2 Tablespoons silken tofu
1/4 cup dates, chopped
3 Tablespoons cold cereal, crushed (for coating)

In a medium-sized bowl, combine shredded wheat, nuts, seeds, and 1 cup cold cereal. In a small saucepan, combine dry sweetener, apple juice concentrate, tofu, and dates, and heat quickly (don't burn it!) for a short time. Add cereal mixture to tofu mixture and mix well.

On a clean surface, roll mixture by teaspoonfuls into small balls and coat with crushed cereal. Place in a container, cover, and refrigerate. Chill for at least 30 minutes before serving.

Store in the refrigerator.

Total Calories Per Snap Using Sunflower Seeds: 69
Total Fat as % of Daily Value: 2%
Protein: 2 gm   Fat: 2 gm   Carbohydrates: 13 gm   Calcium: 41 mg
Iron: 3 mg   Sodium: 42 mg   Dietary Fiber: 1 gm

Breakfast Stacks
(Makes 3 servings)

Imagine peanut butter and jelly meets cornflakes in a pan! This is a good breakfast and a great dessert.

4 Tablespoon silken tofu
1/2 cup soy or rice milk
1/3 cup crushed corn or bran flakes
2 Tablespoons vegan margarine
6 slices bread
2 Tablespoons peanut butter
2 Tablespoons fruit preserves

In a medium-sized bowl mix tofu and milk. Spread cereal on a dinner plate.

Preheat a large frying pan over medium heat and melt margarine. Dip each slice of bread in the milk mixture and cook on one side until golden brown. Remove from pan.

Place non-cooked side of one piece of bread in cereal. Spread cooked side with peanut butter. Set aside. Repeat the same procedure with a second piece of bread, spreading cooked side with fruit preserves. Make a sandwich by pressing the peanut butter and fruit preserve sides together. Return to pan and cook cereal coated sides until heated through and golden brown. Repeat procedure three more times and serve hot.

Total Calories Per Serving Using Soymilk, Bran Flakes, and Raspberry Preserves: 321   Total Fat as % of Daily Value: 26%
Protein: 11 gm   Fat: 17 gm   Carbohydrates: 36 gm   Calcium: 75 mg
Iron: 3 mg   Sodium: 402 mg   Dietary Fiber: 6 gm

Chocolate-on-the-Run

(Makes 1 serving)

Pour this in your thermos, toss a banana and an orange in the knapsack, and you've got a great way to start the day.

2 Tablespoon silken tofu
1 cup soy or rice milk (plain or vanilla are both fine)
1/4 cup dry sweetener
2 Tablespoons unsweetened cocoa powder
1/2 slice whole wheat bread
3 ice cubes

Place all the ingredients in the canister of a blender. Blend on high for 15 seconds or until mixture is slushy. Drink right away or place in the freezer until ready to drink.

Note: This breakfast drink will start "falling apart" after about 10 minutes and will need to be stirred or blended again before consuming.

Total Calories Per Serving Using Plain Soymilk: 350
Total Fat as % of Daily Value: 12%
Protein: 12 gm   Fat: 8 gm   Carbohydrates: 68 gm   Calcium: 44 mg
Iron: 4 mg   Sodium: 107 mg   Dietary Fiber: 1 gm

Latin A.M. Chocolate
(Makes 1 serving)

The cinnamon adds a wonderful accent to this morning chocolate drink.

1-1/2 cups soy or rice milk (plain, vanilla, or chocolate are all fine)
1/8 cup unsweetened cocoa powder
2 Tablespoons dry sweetener
1/4 teaspoon ground cinnamon
1/8 cup boiling water
1/8 teaspoon almond extract

In a small saucepan, heat milk for 3 minutes over medium heat. In a small bowl, combine cocoa powder, dry sweetener, and cinnamon. Add hot water to cocoa and mix thoroughly until there are no lumps. Stir in almond extract. Whisk cocoa mixture into hot milk, pour into a mug and drink hot.

Note: Refrigerate leftovers and reheat in a microwave or on top of a stove. Use as a hot beverage or as a sauce for ice cream, sorbet, or baked items.

Total Calories Per Serving Using Plain Soymilk: 247
Total Fat as % of Daily Value: 13%
Protein: 13 gm   Fat: 9 gm   Carbohydrates: 38 gm   Calcium: 36 mg
Iron: 4 mg   Sodium: 47 mg   Dietary Fiber: 9 gm

Chapter Four

One-Pot Wonders

One-pot dishes have been a traditional part of many cuisines. When fuel and the material to manufacture cooking pots were scarce, it made sense to produce meals that conserved both wood and iron. Think about Japanese hot pot and sukiyaki, Chinese stir-fry, French cassoulet (a baby lima bean and tomato stew), Indian curries, and southwestern chili. These are all one-pot wonders from areas that value both fuel and utensils.

Beyond thrift, one-pot meals allow flavors to marry in wonderful ways. Ingredients allowed to simmer together for extended periods of time unite to create complex yet comforting dishes. You've had this experience, if you've noticed that a dish tastes better the second day, after the flavors have had time to get to know one another.

One-pot meals may take a bit more time with the *mise en place* than, say, preparing sandwiches. But once that initial *mise en place* is completed, these one-pot dishes can usually be left to take care of themselves for a while. Put them on simmer and go put your feet up. You deserve it! And if you play your cards right, there's less water and soap expended during cleanup.

We love to "build a meal." That is, we love to create a meal, hopefully in one pot, but generally in no more than two, using what we've got in the pantry and the refrigerator. Here are some of our favorites:

- "Cream of Dinner:" Take a container of corn soup (We like to use the 15-ounce Imagine Foods aseptically packaged corn soup; it has a great texture and flavor) and get that going on the stove and start building. Add chopped canned tomatoes (with the liquid) and any fresh tomatoes that won't make it another day, canned or frozen corn, firm tofu (cut into chunks), chopped onions, fresh or canned mushrooms, and black pepper and garlic powder. Allow mixture to cook until bubbly hot (and all veggies are soft). Eat right from the pot (we give you permission) or spoon over leftover cooked rice, pasta, mashed potatoes, or whole grain bread. You can use the same ingredients added to tomato or mushroom soup. This will hold in the refrigerator for up to 3 days, can be frozen, or can be eaten cold.

- "Beans Are Us:" Combine up to five different types of (cooked; frozen and thawed; or canned and drained) beans in a medium-sized saucepan. Allow 1 cup of beans for each hearty serving and 3/4 of a cup for an average serving. For chili-style, add canned or fresh chopped tomatoes, prepared salsa, chopped canned or fresh chilies, and chili powder. For curry-style, add plain soy yogurt, some fresh or frozen (thawed) chopped spinach, chopped onions, and curry powder. For Italian-style, add pizza or pasta sauce, sliced mushrooms, leftover cooked pasta, and dried basil, oregano, and garlic. For German-style, add drained sauerkraut, sliced veggie hot dogs, and caraway seeds. Allow to simmer until heated thoroughly and eat as is or on top of rice, pasta, or cornbread.

- Leftover cooked potatoes can be tossed with chunks of plain or flavored tofu, chopped onions, fresh or frozen (thawed) chopped spinach or other shredded greens (such as kale or Swiss chard), pickle relish, and some mayonnaise or silken tofu seasoned with pepper and onion for a fast cold entrée. Use leftover sweet potatoes with crushed pineapple, canned peaches or cherries, chopped nuts and dried fruit, and mayonnaise or silken tofu blended with orange juice concentrate, ground ginger, and cinnamon.

- Bring soup into the picture; in the summer, treat yourself to cool, seasonal soups. Purée avocado with tofu and garlic or fresh peaches, mangos, or apricots with tofu to make fast cold soups. Garnish with chopped fresh herbs, dried fruit or vegetables, fresh berries, or chopped veggies.

- Pasta is the original one-pot wonder. Cook and drain pasta, toss in leftover chopped veggies, olives, chopped onions, peppers, or garlic, shredded greens, shredded vegan soy cheese, and tomato or mushroom sauce, and violá, you have dinner!

I hope you enjoy the following recipes!

Kitchen Sink Minestrone
(Makes 3 servings)

Open the refrigerator and toss a wide variety of ingredients into this soup.

1-1/2 cups vegetable broth or tomato juice
1/4 cup uncooked pasta
3/4 cup frozen mixed vegetables
1 cup canned chopped tomatoes (with juice)
3/4 cup cooked kidney beans
1 teaspoon granulated garlic
1 teaspoon dried basil or 2 teaspoons fresh basil

Place all the ingredients in a medium-sized saucepan. Bring to a boil. Reduce heat, cover, and simmer until pasta is cooked and vegetables are heated through, approximately 20 minutes.

Note: We like to chop firm tofu and toss it into this soup during the last 5 minutes of cooking. Use your leftover fresh and frozen vegetables and beans to add to this soup. If you have leftover cooked pasta, omit the uncooked pasta and add 3/4 cup cooked pasta during the last 10 minutes of cooking.

Total Calories Per Serving Using Vegetable Broth: 134
Total Fat as % of Daily Value: 2%
Protein: 7 gm   Fat: 1 gm   Carbohydrates: 27 gm   Calcium: 122 mg
Iron: 2 mg   Sodium: 564 mg   Dietary Fiber: 3 gm

Corn and Potato Chowder

(Makes 3 servings)

This soup is a hearty meal by itself.

Vegetable oil spray
1/2 cup chopped onions
2 minced garlic cloves
1/8 cup chopped fresh parsley
1-1/4 cups frozen cut corn, thawed or corn cut from
   3 ears of corn
3 cups water
4 cubed boiling potatoes
1 teaspoon dried dill
2 cups soymilk
1 cup silken tofu
1 teaspoon thyme
1/2 teaspoon black pepper

In a large pot, spray vegetable oil and heat. Add onions, garlic, parsley, and corn. Cover the pot and simmer for 20 minutes, stirring frequently. Add water and bring to a boil. Add potatoes and simmer, uncovered, until potatoes are tender, approximately 30 minutes. Stir in dill, soymilk, tofu, thyme, and pepper. Simmer chowder for 15 minutes or until very hot.

Total Calories Per Serving: 309   Total Fat as % of Daily Value: 10%
Protein: 15 gm   Fat: 7 gm   Carbohydrates: 53 gm   Calcium: 75 mg
Iron: 4 mg   Sodium: 39 mg   Dietary Fiber: 8 gm

Cool-As-A-Cucumber Soup
(Makes 2 servings)

Take advantage of the hot weather and don't cook tonight.

1 cup peeled, chopped cucumber
1/2 cup cold vegetable broth
1/4 cup silken tofu
2 Tablespoons chopped green onions
White pepper to taste (about 1/2 teaspoon)
1/8 cup shredded carrots
1 Tablespoon chopped fresh parsley

Place cucumber, broth, tofu, onions, and pepper in a blender. Process until just smooth. Pour into serving bowls and top with carrots and parsley. Chill for at least 30 minutes before serving.

Note: This cold soup is a great light summer entrée and will last for up to 2 days in the refrigerator.

Total Calories Per Serving: 36   Total Fat as % of Daily Value: 2%
Protein: 3 gm   Fat: 1 gm   Carbohydrates: 5 gm   Calcium: 28 mg
Iron: 1 mg   Sodium: 257 mg   Dietary Fiber: 1 gm

Wonder Gazpacho

(Makes 2 servings)

This soup will never miss not being on the stove.

1 cup chopped, ripe tomatoes
2 Tablespoons tomato paste
1/8 cup chopped cucumbers
1/4 cup chopped bell peppers
1/8 cup chopped onions
1 minced garlic clove or 1 teaspoon granulated garlic
1 teaspoon cracked black pepper
2 teaspoons lemon or lime juice

Place all the ingredients in a blender and pulse until a chunky texture is achieved. Pour into serving bowls and chill for at least 30 minutes before serving.

Note: This cold soup can be made spicier by adding salsa or chopped chilies. Serve with breadsticks or crusty French bread, or over cold brown rice or cold, cooked pasta.

Total Calories Per Serving: 48   Total Fat as % of Daily Value: <1%
Protein: 2 gm   Fat: <1 gm   Carbohydrates: 11 gm   Calcium: 23 mg
Iron: 1 mg   Sodium: 24 mg   Dietary Fiber: 3 gm

Salsa Black Bean Salad

(Makes 2 servings)

This salad is dramatic in appearance and taste.

1 cup cooked black beans (if canned, drain and rinse)
1/2 fresh orange, peeled and chopped
1/8 cup chopped green onions
1/4 cup prepared salsa
1 Tablespoon lemon or lime juice
1 minced garlic clove or 1 teaspoon granulated garlic
1 teaspoon cumin
1 teaspoon red pepper flakes
Shredded lettuce, as desired
Tortilla chips or shredded tortillas, as desired

Mix beans, oranges, onions, salsa, juice, garlic, cumin, and pepper flakes together in a medium bowl. Chill for at least 1 hour. Serve over lettuce and garnish with chips.

Total Calories Per Serving Using Lemon Juice (excluding lettuce and tortilla chips): 158   Total Fat as % of Daily Value: 2%
Protein: 9 gm   Fat: 1 gm   Carbohydrates: 30 gm   Calcium: 75 mg
Iron: 3 mg   Sodium: 88 mg   Dietary Fiber: 10 gm

Tangy Tofu Salad
(1 hearty serving or 2 average servings)

Good for the first day, even better the second!

1 Tablespoon olive oil
1/8 cup red wine or balsamic vinegar
1/2 teaspoon dried basil
1/4 teaspoon black pepper
1/4 teaspoon dried oregano
8 ounces firm tofu, cut into medium-sized cubes
3 or 4 lettuce leaves or 1 cup pre-cut salad mix
2 or 3 tomato slices
2 Tablespoons diced onion

In a medium-sized bowl, combine oil, vinegar, basil, pepper, and oregano. Mix to combine. Add tofu, then place in a refrigerator and allow to sit for 15 minutes.

In a salad bowl, combine lettuce, tomatoes, and onions. Add tofu mixture and toss before serving.

Total Calories Per Average Serving: 253
Total Fat as % of Daily Value: 26%
Protein: 19 gm   Fat: 17 gm   Carbohydrates: 9 gm   Calcium: 220 mg
Iron: 13 mg   Sodium: 27 mg   Dietary Fiber: 4 gm

Cucumber Raita

(Makes 3 servings)

Enjoy this cool dish.

1/2 cucumber, peeled and finely chopped
6 ounces plain soy yogurt or soy sour cream (see
glossary)
1/2 teaspoon black pepper
1/4 teaspoon ground cumin

In a small bowl combine all ingredients until well mixed. Chill until
ready to serve.

Total Calories Per Serving: 49   Total Fat as % of Daily Value: 4%
Protein: 3 gm   Fat: 3 gm   Carbohydrates: 4 gm   Calcium: 70 mg
Iron: 3 mg   Sodium: 5 mg   Dietary Fiber: 1 gm

Asian Noodle Bowl
(Makes 2 servings)

Use your leftover cooked noodles for this quick dish.

**1-1/2 cups cooked noodles, chilled (start with 1/2 cup
    uncooked noodles)**
1/4 cup shredded green cabbage
1/8 cup sliced radishes
3/4 cup diced tofu or gluten
2 teaspoons minced fresh garlic
1 teaspoon minced fresh ginger
1 Tablespoon vegetable oil
1 teaspoon soy sauce
2 Tablespoons cashews or peanuts

In a large serving bowl, toss noodles, cabbage, radishes, tofu or
gluten, garlic, and ginger until combined. Add oil and soy sauce.
Mix to combine. Garnish with nuts before serving.

Total Calories Per Serving Using Tofu and Peanuts: 407
Total Fat as % of Daily Value: 31%
Protein: 23 gm   Fat: 20 gm   Carbohydrates: 37 gm   Calcium: 180 mg
Iron: 12 mg   Sodium: 187 mg   Dietary Fiber: 6 gm

Pasta in Paradise
(Makes 2 servings)

This dish is colorful, with an unexpected secret ingredient (psst... it's the mango).

4 ounces uncooked vermicelli, rice noodles, or spaghetti
1/4 cup red or yellow bell pepper strips (about 1 medium pepper)
1 cup ripe chopped papaya (about 1 small papaya)
1 cup ripe chopped tomatoes (about 1 medium tomato)
1/2 cup ripe, chopped mango (about 1 half mango or look for frozen cubes)
2 Tablespoons chopped fresh cilantro or flat leafed parsley
2 teaspoons olive oil
1/4 teaspoon cinnamon
1/2 teaspoon white pepper
2 Tablespoons chopped peanuts

Cook pasta according to package directions. Rinse, drain, and set aside to cool. In a large bowl, combine pepper, papaya, tomatoes, mango, cilantro, oil, cinnamon, and white pepper and toss to mix. Add pasta and toss to mix. Top with peanuts.

Total Calories Per Serving Using Rice Noodles and Cilantro: 376
Total Fat as % of Daily Value: 15%
Protein: 7 gm   Fat: 10 gm   Carbohydrates: 68 gm   Calcium: 44 mg
Iron: 2 mg   Sodium: 19 mg   Dietary Fiber: 4 gm

Pasta Now, Pasta Later
(Makes 4 servings)

Serve this dish the first time as a hot entrée and then as a cold entrée the next day.

Vegetable oil spray
1/4 cup chopped onions
3/4 cup chopped fresh tomatoes (or canned, drained chopped tomatoes)
1/2 cup chopped green or red bell peppers
2 cups cooked pasta (a good place to use up leftovers!)
1/2 cup cooked beans (your choice), drained
1/2 cup frozen corn, thawed (or canned hominy, if you have it)
1 Tablespoon Italian salad dressing (or an oil and vinegar combination)

Heat a large frying pan and spray with oil. Sauté onions, tomatoes, and peppers for 1 minute until slightly wilted. Add pasta, beans, and corn. Toss and cook until heated. Remove from heat, toss with dressing, and eat warm.

Total Calories Per Serving: 160   Total Fat as % of Daily Value: 4%
Protein: 5 gm   Fat: 3 gm   Carbohydrates: 30 gm   Calcium: 20 mg
Iron: 2 mg   Sodium: 137 mg   Dietary Fiber: 3 gm

Comfort Casserole
(Baked Pasta and Peppers)
(Makes 3 servings)

We always make enough for leftovers. This dish is even better the second day.

Vegetable oil spray
**1/2 cup cooked orzo, pastina, or other small-shaped
  pasta**
1/2 cup shredded soy cheese
1/4 cup diced red bell pepper
1/4 cup sliced canned mushrooms, drained
1/2 cup soy sour cream (see glossary)
1 teaspoon pepper
1/2 teaspoon granulated garlic
1/2 teaspoon onion powder
1 Tablespoon vegan margarine

Preheat oven to 400 degrees. Spray a 1-quart (small) baking dish with oil. Combine all ingredients, except margarine, in a baking dish. Dot with margarine. Bake approximately 15 minutes at 400 degrees, uncovered, until golden.

Note: Orzo and pastina are very small pasta shapes, almost resembling rice or grains. They cook up very nicely and can be used for savory dishes, like this one, or even instead of hot cereal, in the morning.

Total Calories Per Serving: 114   Total Fat as % of Daily Value: 9%
Protein: 5 gm   Fat: 8 gm   Carbohydrates: 12 gm   Calcium: 46 mg
Iron: 1 mg   Sodium: 121 mg   Dietary Fiber: 1 gm

Sufferin' Sweet Potato Succotash
(Makes 3 servings)

This dish is so easy to make and fun to eat.

1-1/2 cups frozen cut corn, thawed
3/4 cup frozen lima beans, thawed
Vegetable oil spray
1/3 cup diced onion
1 minced garlic clove
10-ounce can sweet potatoes, drained and diced or
    1-1/4 cups diced baked sweet potato
1 teaspoon white pepper

In a small bowl, toss together corn and lima beans. Set aside.
    Spray a medium-sized pot with oil. Heat and sauté onions and garlic until soft, approximately 2 minutes. Add corn, limas, sweet potatoes, and pepper. Cook for 5 minutes or until all veggies are hot.

Total Calories Per Serving: 200   Total Fat as % of Daily Value: 2%
Protein: 7 gm   Fat: 1 gm   Carbohydrates: 44 gm   Calcium: 49 mg
Iron: 2 mg   Sodium: 24 mg   Dietary Fiber: 7 gm

Garlic and Rosemary Sweet Potatoes

(Makes 2 servings)

The kitchen smells wonderful while this recipe is baking.

1 large sweet potato (about 1 pound)
1 teaspoon dried rosemary
1 teaspoon granulated garlic
1 Tablespoon melted vegan margarine or oil

Preheat oven to 425 degrees. Peel potato and cut into wedges.
Toss potato with rosemary and garlic. Arrange potatoes in a
single layer on a baking sheet. Drizzle with margarine or oil.
Bake at 425 degrees for 30 to 40 minutes, turning at least once,
until potatoes are tender. Serve warm.

Total Calories Per Serving: 146   Total Fat as % of Daily Value: 9%
Protein: 2 gm   Fat: 6 gm   Carbohydrates: 22 gm   Calcium: 30 mg
Iron: 1 mg   Sodium: 78 mg   Dietary Fiber: 3 gm

Spicy Pepper-Corn and Coconut Milk
(Makes 2 servings)

Here's a 'taste of the Islands' in your own kitchen.

Vegetable oil spray
2 chopped green onions
1 seeded and chopped fresh chili or 1 Tablespoon red
  pepper flakes
1 minced garlic clove
1/4 cup chopped fresh tomato
1/4 cup chopped green or red bell pepper
2 teaspoons black pepper
1/4 teaspoon dried thyme
1-1/4 cups frozen cut corn, thawed or 3 ears fresh corn
  cut from cob
1/3 cup canned unsweetened coconut milk

Heat a medium-sized pot and spray with oil. Sauté onions, chili, and garlic until onions are soft, approximately 3 minutes. Add tomato, bell pepper, and black pepper. Cook, stirring, until veggies are soft and most of the liquid is absorbed, approximately 5 minutes. Add thyme, corn, and coconut milk. Lower heat to simmer, and cook, uncovered, for 10 minutes or until thickened. Eat while hot.

Total Calories Per Serving: 191   Total Fat as % of Daily Value: 14%
Protein: 5 gm   Fat: 9 gm   Carbohydrates: 28 gm   Calcium: 40 mg
Iron: 3 mg   Sodium: 17 mg   Dietary Fiber: 5 gm

Crank Up the Heat Rice and Beans
(Makes 2 servings)

You choose your heat on this one.

1 cup cooked red or kidney beans (canned beans are fine), drained
1/2 cup tomato juice
1/4 cup crumbled smoked fake meat strips, soy sausage, or smoked tempeh
1/4 cup minced onions
1/4 cup minced green bell pepper
1/4 cup chopped fresh tomatoes
1 minced garlic clove
1 fresh seeded and minced fresh chili (you choose the heat)
1 cup uncooked white rice
1 cup vegetable broth
2 teaspoons hot sauce

Place beans in a medium-sized pot and allow to simmer for 1 minute. Add tomato juice, fake meat strips, soy sausage, or smoked tempeh, onion, bell pepper, tomatoes, garlic, and chili and simmer for 20 minutes (do not allow mixture to dry out). Stir in rice, broth, and hot sauce. Bring to a quick boil, reduce heat, cover and cook for 20 minutes or until all the liquid is absorbed and the rice is soft. Eat while hot.

Total Calories Per Serving Using Red Kidney Beans and Tempeh: 389
Total Fat as % of Daily Value: 4%
Protein: 15 gm   Fat: 2 gm   Carbohydrates: 78 gm   Calcium: 33 mg
Iron: 2 mg   Sodium: 366 mg   Dietary Fiber: 11 gm

Lentil-Spinach Pilaf
(Makes 3 servings)

Use canned lentils to really speed up the preparation of this dish.

Vegetable oil spray
2 cups chopped fresh spinach or 1 cup frozen chopped
**   spinach, thawed and drained**
1 minced garlic clove
3/4 cup cooked lentils (start with 1/3 cup uncooked
**   lentils; canned, drained, lentils are fine, too)**
1 Tablespoon chopped fresh parsley or 2 teaspoons
**   dried parsley**
1/4 teaspoon cumin
1/4 teaspoon pepper

Spray a large frying pan with oil and heat. Add spinach and garlic. Cook, stirring, until spinach is wilted and hot, approximately 2 minutes. Add lentils, parsley, cumin, and pepper. Stir until heated through, approximately 3 minutes. Do not overcook, as the spinach will lose its terrific flavor and texture.

Note: Cooked soy beans, butter beans (baby limas), and white beans may be used instead of or in combination with the lentils.

Total Calories Per Serving: 72   Total Fat as % of Daily Value: 1%
Protein: 6 gm   Fat: 1 gm   Carbohydrates: 12 gm   Calcium: 52 mg
Iron: 3 mg   Sodium: 32 mg   Dietary Fiber: 5 gm

Garbs and Carbs
(Makes 2 servings)

This dish is colorful, crunchy, and delicious!

1-1/2 cups canned garbanzo beans, drained
1/2 cup chopped celery
1/2 peeled and chopped cucumber
1/4 cup chopped carrots
1/2 cup chopped raw zucchini or yellow squash
1 chopped green onion
2 Tablespoons chopped fresh parsley
1/8 cup vinegar
2 teaspoons lemon juice
2 teaspoons oil
1/8 teaspoon black pepper

In a medium-sized bowl, toss all the ingredients. Allow dish to cool. Then marinate for at least 1 hour before eating.

If you'd like a dressing with your garb salad, the recipe for Cucumber Raita on page 65 is a way to use up the other half of the cucumber. The raita also goes well with fiery dishes, such as the Cauliflower Curry later in this chapter.

Total Calories Per Serving Using Zucchini: 247
Total Fat as % of Daily Value: 13%
Protein: 9 gm   Fat: 8 gm   Carbohydrates: 37 gm   Calcium: 97 mg
Iron: 4 mg   Sodium: 457 mg   Dietary Fiber: 12 gm

Hoppin' John
(Makes 3 servings)

Here's a new spin on this traditional New Year's dish.

2-1/2 cups water
3/4 cup dried or fresh black-eyed peas
2 teaspoons onion powder
1 teaspoon granulated garlic
1/3 cup uncooked white rice
1/4 teaspoon thyme
2 teaspoons vegan margarine
4 ounces smoked tofu or seitan, diced
1 teaspoon hot sauce

In a medium-sized saucepan, bring the water to a boil. Add black-eyed peas and boil for 1 minute. Add onion and garlic powder, reduce heat, cover, and simmer for 45 minutes or until the black-eyed peas are just tender. Stir in rice, thyme, margarine, and tofu or seitan. Bring to a boil, reduce heat, cover, and allow dish to simmer for approximately 20 minutes or until all the liquid is absorbed. Add hot sauce right before eating.

Total Calories Per Serving Using Tofu: 194
Total Fat as % of Daily Value: 9%
Protein: 9 gm   Fat: 6 gm   Carbohydrates: 27 gm   Calcium: 119 mg
Iron: 5 mg   Sodium: 39 mg   Dietary Fiber: 4 gm

Put Together in Ten Minutes Casserole
(Makes 2 servings)

You can probably prepare this casserole in even less time!

1/2 cup chopped celery
1/4 cup chopped onions
1 Tablespoon soy sauce
1 teaspoon granulated garlic
1/2 teaspoon ground ginger
3/4 cup diced firm tofu, tempeh, or seitan
10-ounce can vegan mushroom soup
1/3 cup frozen peas
1/2 cup vegan chow mein noodles (the crunchy ones)

Preheat oven to 350 degrees. In a baking dish, combine all ingredients except chow mein noodles. Mix until combined. Top with noodles and bake at 350 degrees for approximately 45 minutes or until lightly browned and bubbly.

Note: Dare we tell you that if no chow mein noodles are to be found, you can use smashed potato or corn chips?

Total Calories Per Serving Using Tofu: 293
Total Fat as % of Daily Value: 22%
Protein: 20 gm   Fat: 15 gm   Carbohydrates: 25 gm   Calcium: 218 mg
Iron: 12 mg   Sodium: 1187 mg   Dietary Fiber: 6 gm

Raisins and Brown Rice

(Makes 3 servings)

Enjoy this kind of sweet, kind of savory dish.

1-1/2 cups water
1/2 cup uncooked brown rice
1/4 cup raisins
1/4 cup slivered or chopped almonds
2 teaspoons onion powder
1 teaspoon dried parsley
1/8 teaspoon cinnamon
1 teaspoon vegan margarine

In a medium-sized saucepan, bring water to a boil. Add rice, raisins, almonds, onions, parsley, and cinnamon. Reduce heat, cover, and cook for approximately 45 minutes or until liquid is absorbed. Stir in margarine and serve hot.

Total Calories Per Serving: 220   Total Fat as % of Daily Value: 10%
Protein: 5 gm   Fat: 6 gm   Carbohydrates: 37 gm   Calcium: 44 mg
Iron: 1 mg   Sodium: 20 mg   Dietary Fiber: 3 gm

Sweet Indian Rice
with Carrots and Dates
(Makes 2 servings)

Pair this with a garlicky salad or a tangy bean dish (or eat it on its own).

2 Tablespoons vegan margarine
1 cup matchstick cut peeled carrots
2 Tablespoons chopped dates
1-1/2 cups vegetable broth
1/2 teaspoon cinnamon
1/2 teaspoon nutmeg
1/2 teaspoon ground cloves
1/4 teaspoon ground cardamom
3/4 cup uncooked white or basmati rice

Melt margarine in a large pot. Add carrots and dates; cook and stir until carrots are soft, approximately 5 minutes. Add broth and spices, stir, and bring to a quick boil. Reduce heat and simmer until rice is cooked and all the liquid is absorbed, approximately 20 minutes.

Total Calories Per Serving: 446   Total Fat as % of Daily Value: 21%
Protein: 8 gm   Fat: 14 gm   Carbohydrates: 76 gm   Calcium: 40 mg
Iron: 1 mg   Sodium: 910 mg   Dietary Fiber: 5 gm

Wild Rice Pilaf
with Celery and Carrots
(Makes 3 servings)

Try using fennel, which will give a slightly anise or licorice flavor to the rice.

1-1/2 quarts water
1 cup wild rice
Vegetable oil spray
3 stalks celery, chopped (or 1 fresh fennel bulb, in season)
3/4 cup matchstick cut peeled carrots
1/2 cup chopped onion
3/4 cup long grain white rice or converted rice
1 teaspoon thyme
1 teaspoon tarragon
2 cups vegetable broth
1/2 cup white wine (or use 1/2 cup more broth)

In a large pot, boil water. Add wild rice and boil for 10 minutes. Drain well and set aside. In the same pot, generously spray oil and allow to heat. Add celery and carrots. Cook and stir for 4 minutes. Add onion. Cook and stir for 3 minutes, until vegetables are beginning to get soft. Add cooked wild rice and uncooked white rice. Stir to coat with veggies and oil. Mix in thyme, tarragon, broth, and wine. Bring to a fast boil, reduce heat, cover, and allow to simmer for 40 minutes, or until all liquid is absorbed.

Total Calories Per Serving: 434   Total Fat as % of Daily Value: 3%
Protein: 14 gm   Fat: 2 gm   Carbohydrates: 86 gm   Calcium: 72 mg
Iron: 4 mg   Sodium: 721 mg   Dietary Fiber: 6 gm

Quick Cajun Rice and Beans

(Makes 2 servings)

Chef Paul never made this dish so fast!

Vegetable oil spray
1/2 cup chopped onions
1/2 cup chopped green bell pepper
1 minced garlic clove
1/2 cup (4 ounces) soy sausage or soy crumbles
1 cup canned chopped tomatoes
1 cup vegetable broth
1 cup instant rice (such as Minute Rice)
1/2 teaspoon black pepper
1/2 teaspoon thyme
1/2 teaspoon oregano
1 cup canned white beans (such as Great Northern or butter beans), drained
1 cup canned red beans, (such as Kidney beans) drained
Tabasco or hot sauce, as desired

Heat a large pot and spray with oil. Add onion, bell pepper, and garlic and sauté until soft, approximately 2 minutes. Add soy sausage or crumbles and cook for 1 minute. Add tomatoes, broth, and rice. Bring to a fast boil, reduce heat to simmer, and add black pepper, thyme, and oregano. Cover pot and cook for 4 minutes. Stir in beans and continue to cook until beans are hot and all liquid is absorbed. Add Tabasco and serve.

Total Calories Per Serving: 475   Total Fat as % of Daily Value: 7%
Protein: 25 gm   Fat: 4 gm   Carbohydrates: 87 gm   Calcium: 156 mg
Iron: 7 mg   Sodium: 750 mg   Dietary Fiber: 21 gm

Asian Cabbage and Green Onions

(Makes 2 servings)

Take advantage of pre-cut cabbage for this dish. Look for bags of coleslaw mix in the produce section (the slaw mix may contain some red cabbage or carrots; that just adds to the flavor).

1 Tablespoon oil (if you want Asian authenticity, use peanut or sesame oil)
1-1/2 cups pre-shredded cabbage (or about 1 small head, it you are chopping it)
4 green onions, sliced into 1-inch lengths
1/2 cup vegetable broth
1 Tablespoon soy sauce
2 Tablespoons white vinegar (for authenticity, use rice vinegar)
1 Tablespoon dry sweetener
1 teaspoon red pepper flakes

Heat oil in a wok or medium-sized frying pan. Add cabbage and onions and sauté over medium heat until the cabbage is wilted, approximately 2 minutes. Reduce heat and add broth, soy sauce, vinegar, sweetener, and red pepper. Stir to combine. Cook for 5 minutes longer or until cabbage and onions are soft. Eat immediately.

Total Calories Per Serving Using Sesame Oil and White Rice Vinegar: 122
Total Fat as % of Daily Value: 12%
Protein: 3 gm   Fat: 7 gm   Carbohydrates: 13 gm   Calcium: 46 mg
Iron: 1 mg   Sodium: 767 mg   Dietary Fiber: 3 gm

Zucchini, Green Bean, and Potato Stew
(Makes 2 servings)

Enjoy this delicious stew.

Vegetable oil spray
1/4 cup chopped onions
1 cup cut green beans (fresh or thawed frozen)
1/4 teaspoon red pepper flakes
1/2 cup sliced zucchini (fresh or thawed frozen)
1 cup baking potato, peeled and cubed
1/4 cup chopped fresh parsley
1-1/2 cups chopped canned tomatoes, not drained (or
    use one 8-ounce can)

Heat a large frying pan and spray with oil. Add onions and sauté until soft, approximately 2 minutes. Add green beans and pepper flakes and continue to sauté until onions are translucent, approximately 3 minutes. Add zucchini, potato, and parsley, and toss to mix. Add tomatoes. Bring to a fast boil, lower heat, cover, and simmer, stirring frequently, until potatoes are tender, approximately 40 minutes.

Total Calories Per Serving: 129   Total Fat as % of Daily Value: 2%
Protein: 5 gm   Fat: 1 gm   Carbohydrates: 28 gm   Calcium: 97 mg
Iron: 2 mg   Sodium: 279 mg   Dietary Fiber: 6 gm

Cauliflower Curry
(Makes 2 servings)

Actually, this could be broccoli, Brussels sprout, cooked cubed potato, green or wax bean, mixed veggie, or okra curry, depending on your preference. This recipe looks like a lot of work; however, it should only take about 30 minutes to prepare.

1 Tablespoon olive oil
1/4 cup thinly sliced onion
2 minced garlic cloves
2 Tablespoons minced fresh ginger (you really need fresh ginger for this recipe)
1 seeded and minced Jalapeño or serrano chili (you choose the heat; if you want it really mild, use 2 Tablespoons of green bell pepper)
2 teaspoons curry powder
1 cup frozen or fresh cauliflower florets (or veggie of your choice)
1/2 cup unsweetened coconut milk (be sure to buy coconut milk, not coconut cream)
2 teaspoons lemon juice

Heat oil in a large skillet. Add onion, garlic, ginger, and chili and sauté until lightly browned, approximately 5 minutes. Add curry powder, stirring for 3 minutes. Add cauliflower, coconut milk, and lemon juice, reduce heat to simmer, and allow to cook for approximately 5 minutes or until heated through.

Note: If you'd like to make a more authentic curry, mix your own curry powder with 1 teaspoon ground coriander, 1/2 teaspoon cumin, 1/4 teaspoon cinnamon, 1/2 teaspoon turmeric, and 1/4 teaspoon black mustard seed.

Total Calories Per Serving: 106   Total Fat as % of Daily Value: 12%
Protein: 2 gm   Fat: 8 gm   Carbohydrates: 9 gm   Calcium: 47 mg
Iron: 1 mg   Sodium: 47 mg   Dietary Fiber: 2 gm

Is it Tofu? Is it Tempeh? It's Garlic, For Sure

(Makes 2 hearty servings)

This dish is guaranteed to keep vampires away. Use this as a sandwich stuffing (good hot or cold) or serve over cooked noodles (how about spinach or carrot pasta), steamed rice, or over a baked potato.

2 Tablespoons olive oil (any vegetable oil is okay)
2 Tablespoons minced garlic cloves
3 Tablespoons flour
1 cup soymilk
1/2 teaspoon black pepper
3/4 cup cubed firm tofu or tempeh

In a medium-sized frying pan, heat oil. Add garlic and sauté until garlic is lightly browned. Remove from heat and whisk in flour to make a paste.

Heat soymilk in a microwave or in a small pot until bubbly. Slowly add paste to soymilk, whisking, to form a smooth sauce, over low heat, approximately 5 minutes. Add tofu or tempeh and allow dish to cook for 3-4 minutes, until heated.

Note: You can try flavored tofu or tempeh, such as barbecue, smoked, or Cajun to add even more flavor.

Total Calories Per Serving Using Tofu: 353
Total Fat as % of Daily Value: 37%
Protein: 20 gm   Fat: 24 gm   Carbohydrates: 18 gm   Calcium: 177 mg
Iron: 12 mg   Sodium: 30 mg   Dietary Fiber: 4 gm

Freeze or Refrigerate Now, Eat Later

There are days when you feel like cooking and days when you don't. Sometimes you have the time to prepare a wonderful meal and sometimes it seems like it's too much to open a can of soup. Let's face it, we've all done the cold-cereal-for-supper routine.

There are certainly lots of convenience items available (fresh, frozen, or canned), which you can stock up with for those days. Sometimes doing a little shopping is a pleasant segue from work or classes to home. And sometimes you'd rather go to the gym, hang out at the local coffee house, go for a walk, or spend some time reading, anything but have to think about dinner. On those days, wouldn't it be nice if meals just materialized?

With a little planning, you can be pretty close to having meals appear on your table. If you can set aside some time every couple of weeks for shopping and cooking, you can have a selection of hand-tailored meals waiting in your freezer. Then, when the world has stomped on you (or you just get too involved in a good book or computer game), you know you have the comfort of a home-cooked meal waiting for you. In fact, if you like, you can do enough prepare-ahead cooking to have the occasional spontaneous brunch or dinner get-together.

Your freezer food will become a treasure chest, literally. You can feed yourself (and your friends, if you choose) at a moment's notice. You will have meals made with ingredients that you have selected (so you know where they came from and what they're made of). The dishes will be low in the things you may want them low in (such as salt, fat, and preservatives) and high in what you may want them high in (such as fiber, iron, and vitamins). And your budget will thank you, as your own personal convenience foods will cost a lot less than store-bought convenience foods. Who knows? You might start a food business of your own!

You don't need any special equipment to cook-and-freeze, although you want to be sure you have lots of containers to freeze in. Your containers can be recycled food containers (be sure they are not single-use containers, such as some microwaveable containers are; just look on the label for this information), Tupperware-type containers, plastic food bags, or glass containers. Avoid metal, as there can be a reaction between the food and the metal. This pertains to aluminum foil, as well. Foil is soft and some of the metal can be absorbed by the food. Be sure your storage containers are sanitized, which means hand wash them with antibacterial soap and hot water (and allow to air-dry) or run them through a dishwasher with a sanitizing rinse.

Allow food to thaw in the refrigerator. Some foods don't need to be thawed before cooking, such as pizza or soup, but some benefit from thawing first. Never allow food to sit out at room temperature, as bacteria which can cause food-borne illness grows very well at temperatures above 40 degrees Fahrenheit.

The following are recipes that you can prepare and freeze for later use.

Freezer Pizza
(Makes 1 serving)

Pizza freezes well, is a great item to use leftovers, reheats quickly, and makes a fast breakfast (yes, we all do this sometime!), lunch, supper, or snack. We've given you a basic recipe; use your imagination (and your leftovers) to expand on it. Pizza crust can be purchased ready-to-use, ready-to-bake, or as a dry mix. You decide which one is most convenient for you. And, of course, you can always use English muffins or bagels instead of crust.

6-inch prepared pizza crust
1/2 cup prepared pizza sauce (or canned tomato sauce or salsa mixed with 1 Tablespoon tomato paste)
1/8 cup chopped onions
1/8 cup chopped bell peppers
4 thin slices fresh tomato
1 teaspoon dried basil or 2 teaspoons fresh basil
1 teaspoon dried oregano or 2 teaspoon fresh oregano
2 teaspoons fresh minced garlic or 1 teaspoon granulated garlic

Preheat oven to 400 degrees. Spread sauce evenly on crust. Evenly place onions, peppers, and tomatoes on top of sauce. Sprinkle basil, oregano, and garlic on top of vegetables. Bake pizza at 400 degrees for 5 minutes or until vegetables are heated through. Allow to cool thoroughly, then freeze as a whole pizza (a 6-inch pizza is approximately 4 slices) or as individual slices. Remember to label!

Total Calories Per Pizza Using Fresh Herbs: 859
Total Fat as % of Daily Value: 19%
Protein: 29 gm   Fat: 12 gm   Carbohydrates: 160 gm   Calcium: 104 mg
Iron: 10 mg   Sodium: 2124 mg   Dietary Fiber: 9 gm

Here are some pizza-combination ideas to add to the basic pizza:

♦ <u>Potato, spinach, and onion</u>: add cooked, sliced or chopped potatoes (some of those hash browns left over from breakfast!), torn raw spinach leaves, and thinly sliced onions to the basic pizza. Drizzle with a small amount of olive oil, if desired. Bake for approximately 8 minutes or until heated.

♦ <u>Artichoke, mushroom, and rosemary</u>: chop canned artichoke hearts, slice fresh button mushrooms, and add to pizza. Add 1 teaspoon dried rosemary to basil and oregano.

♦ <u>Roasted veggie</u>: if you put on the oven or the barbecue, slice and roast or grill onions, carrots, bell peppers, zucchini or summer squash, mushrooms, and potatoes. Use these as additional toppings.

♦ <u>Sun-dried tomato and pineapple</u>: slice sun-dried tomatoes into thin strips and drain and chop canned pineapple. Use as additional toppings.

♦ <u>Smoky pizza</u>: purchase soy or vegetable breakfast strips or smoke-flavored fake meats. Add these and additional sliced tomatoes to the basic pizza.

Smoky Black Beans
(Makes about 4 hearty servings)

This recipe actually improves when made ahead of time and reheated; all the flavors meld.

2 cups cooked black beans, drained (canned beans are fine)
1/4 cup chopped onions
1 Tablespoon oil or margarine
1 minced garlic clove or 2 teaspoons granulated garlic
1 teaspoon dried oregano
1 fresh seeded and chopped jalapeño or 2 Tablespoons fresh chili or pepper of your choice (you choose the heat)
8 ounces vegan soy sausage (we like Soyrizo or Mexican-flavored soy sausage)
2 teaspoon minced fresh cilantro (or fresh flat-leafed parsley will do)

In a medium-sized pot, combine beans and onions and heat for 5 minutes to combine flavors. In a separate pot, heat oil and sauté garlic for 1 minute. Add bean mixture, oregano, and chili. Reduce heat, cover, and allow to simmer.

While beans are simmering, heat a small frying pan and cook vegan sausage (you shouldn't need any oil). Heat sausage, stirring until it is hot and crumbled. Add to beans. Allow dish to cook for 10 minutes, covered. Serve warm or allow to cool before freezing.

Note: If cooking your own beans, place approximately 3/4 cup uncooked beans in about 1-1/2 quarts of water. Soyrizo is sometimes available in the refrigerated section of the store and it's well worth looking for; if not available, choose smoky or barbecue-flavored soy sausage or soy crumbles. If none of these are available, you can use smoky-flavored seitan or even thinly sliced fake meat deli slices. Also, if you can't find Soyrizo in your market, go to www.friedas.com, a specialty produce company that stocks a lot of soy products which are nationally distributed.

Total Calories Per Serving: 209   Total Fat as % of Daily Value: 7%
Protein: 18 gm   Fat: 5 gm   Carbohydrates: 26 gm   Calcium: 88 mg
Iron: 4 mg   Sodium: 759 mg   Dietary Fiber: 11 gm

Dahl
(Makes 3 servings)

Rice and dahl are the universal condiments to all Indian dishes. There are many different varieties. Here is an easy one.

3/4 cup yellow lentils
3 cups vegetable broth
1/4 cup chopped tomato
1/2 teaspoon turmeric
Vegetable oil spray
1/2 cup chopped onions
1 minced garlic clove
1/8 cup chopped red pepper or fresh red chili
1/2 teaspoon curry powder
1 teaspoon fresh cilantro

In a medium-sized pot, combine lentils, broth, tomato, and turmeric and bring to a fast boil. Reduce heat, cover, and allow mixture to simmer until lentils are soft, approximately 30 minutes.
   Spray a medium-sized frying pan with oil. Add onions, garlic, pepper or chili, curry, and cilantro and cook over a medium heat until onions are translucent, approximately 20 minutes. Add lentil mixture to onions, bring to a boil, reduce heat, and allow dahl to simmer for 5 minutes. Serve warm or cool before freezing.

Total Calories Per Serving: 208   Total Fat as % of Daily Value: 3%
Protein: 16 gm   Fat: 2 gm   Carbohydrates: 35 gm   Calcium: 37 mg
Iron: 5 mg   Sodium: 1008 mg   Dietary Fiber: 16 gm

Beet and Dill Pancakes

(Makes about ten 4-inch pancakes)

Prepare this savory batter and freeze the batter (uncooked) for later use or you can also freeze the cooked pancakes and reheat them.

1-1/2 cups all purpose flour
2 teaspoons baking powder
1 cup plain soymilk
2 Tablespoons silken tofu
3 Tablespoons olive oil or melted vegan margarine
2 Tablespoons minced fresh dill or 1 Tablespoon dried
  dill
1-1/2 cups canned beets, drained and cut into thin
  strips
Vegetable oil spray

Sift flour and baking powder together in a medium-sized bowl. In a separate bowl, beat soymilk, tofu, oil, and dill together until well combined. Slowly add liquid to dry ingredients, whisking until well combined. Mix in beets. Cover and refrigerate for at least 2 hours or freeze for later use.

  Heat a large skillet over medium heat and spray with oil. Slightly stir batter. If it is too thick, thin with more soymilk. Pour 1/4 cup of batter at a time onto the skillet. When bubbles appear on each pancake, flip and allow them to cook on other side until golden brown. Serve hot, with margarine, dill, and extra beets, if desired.

Note: If you'd like to use fresh beets instead of canned, purchase about 3 medium beets and cook them in water (to cover) until easily pierced with a fork. Peel and grate.

Total Calories Per Serving Using Oil: 123   Total Fat as % of Daily Value: 8%
Protein: 3 gm   Fat: 5 gm   Carbohydrates: 17 gm   Calcium: 63 mg
Iron: 2 mg   Sodium: 147 mg   Dietary Fiber: 1 gm

Stuffed Peppers
(Makes 4 peppers)

Use your imagination when seasoning and flavoring the stuffing!

4 medium green bell peppers
1 cup uncooked brown rice or barley
2 cups vegetable broth or water
2 Tablespoons tomato juice
1 Tablespoon red wine or red vinegar
1/2 cup silken tofu
1/2 cup dried cranberries or raisins
1/4 cup chopped walnuts, almonds, or pine nuts
1 teaspoon black pepper
1 teaspoon ground ginger

Preheat oven to 350 degrees. Cut off pepper tops and remove seeds. Put peppers in a small baking pan (glass is better, but metal will work) with 1 inch of cold water.

In a small pan, mix rice and broth or water. Cover, bring to a boil, reduce heat, and allow mixture to simmer until rice is tender, approximately 40 minutes.

In a small frying pan, heat tomato juice and wine together, simmering for 2 minutes. Add tofu and continue to heat, stirring, until liquid is absorbed, approximately 5 minutes.

In a medium-sized bowl, combine cooked rice, cranberries, nuts, pepper, ginger, and tofu. Mix well. Stuff by firmly pressing filling into peppers and bake, covered, at 350 degrees for 15 minutes, or until peppers are soft and filling is heated.

Note: You don't have to limit yourself to green bell peppers; yellow and red peppers, onions, tomatoes, and even small eggplant or summer squash work just as well.

Total Calories Per Pepper: 333   Total Fat as % of Daily Value: 12%
Protein: 8 gm   Fat: 8 gm   Carbohydrates: 59 gm   Calcium: 42 mg
Iron: 2 mg   Sodium: 509 mg   Dietary Fiber: 6 gm

Better Than Beef Stew

(Makes 4 servings)

With its hearty flavor, this recipe will warm you up during the cold months.

3/4 cup cubed onions
4 peeled carrots, thickly sliced
1 cup washed and thickly sliced button mushrooms
2 baking potatoes, peeled and cubed
3 minced garlic cloves
1 cup vegetable broth
1/4 cup tomato paste
1/4 cup white wine or 1/4 cup vegetable broth plus
    1 Tablespoon vinegar
1 Tablespoon dried parsley
1 pound tempeh or seitan (flavored is okay), cubed

Preheat oven to 350 degrees.

    Place all ingredients, except tempeh or seitan, in a medium-sized roasting pan. Cover and allow mixture to cook at 350 degrees until all veggies are tender, at least 1 hour. Add tempeh, recover, and allow dish to stew for an additional 30 minutes.

Total Calories Per Serving Using Tempeh: 379
Total Fat as % of Daily Value: 15%
Protein: 26 gm   Fat: 9gm   Carbohydrates: 52 gm   Calcium: 152 mg
Iron: 4 mg   Sodium: 305 mg   Dietary Fiber: 11 gm

Power Chili
(Makes 4 servings)

Better yet, call this Chili with the Works!

Vegetable oil spray
2 minced garlic cloves
1/2 cup diced onions
1/4 cup diced green bell pepper
1/4 cup diced red bell pepper
1/2 cup soy sausage (Soyrizo is good, as are smoky-flavored sausage)
1/2 cup frozen cut corn, thawed
1-1/2 cups cooked beans, drained (canned are fine; use different varieties)
1 cup vegetable broth
2 teaspoons chili powder
1 teaspoon red pepper flakes
1/2 teaspoon cumin

Heat a large pot and spray with oil. Add garlic, onions, and peppers and sauté until soft. Add sausage and sauté until cooked, approximately 3 minutes. Be sure to crumble sausage. Add remaining ingredients and bring to a fast boil. Reduce heat, allow to simmer until veggies are tender, approximately 30 minutes. The longer this chili cooks, the more flavorful it becomes. Serve warm or freeze for later use.

Total Calories Per Serving Using Red Kidney Beans: 174
Total Fat as % of Daily Value: 4%
Protein: 10 gm   Fat: 3gm   Carbohydrates: 31 gm   Calcium: 20 mg
Iron: 1 mg   Sodium: 351 mg   Dietary Fiber: 11 gm

Vegetables Provencale
(Makes 4 servings)

This is a colorful, flavorful dish, reminiscent of southern France.

Vegetable oil spray
1 minced garlic clove
1 Tablespoon tomato paste
1 cup cubed zucchini
1/2 pound cubed eggplant (not peeled)
1 cup cubed ripe tomatoes
1/2 cup chopped red bell pepper
1/4 cup chopped red onion
1/2 cup sliced fresh mushrooms
2 Tablespoons chopped fresh parsley
1 Tablespoon dried basil
1/2 teaspoon dried thyme
1/2 teaspoon dried rosemary

Spray a medium-sized frying pan with oil and allow to heat. Add garlic and sauté for 1 minute. Stir in tomato paste and immediately add zucchini, eggplant, tomatoes, bell pepper, onions, and mushrooms. Cover and cook until veggies are tender, approximately 15 minutes. Combine seasonings and stir into vegetables. Allow to cook for 1 more minute. Eat while hot or refrigerate until ready to eat. You can also freeze this dish.

Note: Herbes de Provence is a seasoning blend that includes many herbs and spices, including thyme and lavender. You can use 3 Tablespoons of herbes de Provence to replace the listed seasonings. Many markets sell this blend with all the other spices.

Total Calories Per Serving: 52   Total Fat as % of Daily Value: 1%
Protein: 2 gm   Fat: 1 gm   Carbohydrates: 11 gm   Calcium: 50 mg
Iron: 2 mg   Sodium: 13 mg   Dietary Fiber: 4 gm

Green and Creamy Soup
(Makes 4 servings)

Use this freezeable soup as part of a hearty meal or as a sauce for rice, potatoes, barley, or steamed or roasted veggies.

Vegetable oil spray
1/2 cup chopped onion
1/4 cup celery
3 cups vegetable broth
1/4 cup dried split peas, rinsed
1 bay leaf
1 cup diced zucchini or yellow squash (thawed, frozen squash will work)
1/2 teaspoon dried basil
1 cup thawed, frozen chopped spinach, drained
1 Tablespoon chopped fresh parsley

Heat a medium-sized saucepan and spray with oil. Sauté onions and celery until soft, approximately 2 minutes. Add vegetable broth, split peas, and bay leaf. Bring to a quick boil, reduce heat, and cover. Simmer for 30 minutes. Add squash and basil and simmer for 5 minutes. Remove bay leaf and place soup in a blender. Blend until smooth. Put soup back in pot, add spinach and parsley, and heat for 5 minutes. Serve soup hot or allow it to cool before freezing.

Total Calories Per Serving: 84   Total Fat as % of Daily Value: 2%
Protein: 6 gm   Fat: 2 gm   Carbohydrates: 15 gm   Calcium: 67 mg
Iron: 2 mg   Sodium: 793 mg   Dietary Fiber: 4 gm

Balsamic Tomato Soup or Sauce

(Makes 4 servings)

Use this dish as a refreshing cold soup during hot weather or heat as a delicate sauce for veggies, pasta, or tofu.

1-1/2 pounds very ripe tomatoes
1 Tablespoon olive oil (other oils are okay, but won't give the fullest of flavor)
2 teaspoons balsamic vinegar (red wine vinegar is okay, but won't give the fullest of flavor)
1 teaspoon dried oregano
1 teaspoon black pepper

Blanch tomatoes by submerging them in boiling water for 1 minute and then submerging them in ice water to cool. This is to make peeling easy. If the tomatoes already seem easy to peel, you can skip this step. Core and peel tomatoes. Cut in half and, holding a half in your hand, gently squeeze out seeds. Discard seeds.

Place tomatoes in a blender or food processor and process until puréed. Add oil, vinegar, oregano, and pepper and blend to combine. Refrigerate for at least 2 hours before serving. This can be frozen until ready to eat.

Note: You can add leftover chopped veggies to make cold vegetable soup. This dish can even be used as a cold salad dressing.

Total Calories Per Serving: 70   Total Fat as % of Daily Value: 6%
Protein: 2 gm   Fat: 4 gm   Carbohydrates: 9 gm   Calcium: 98 mg
Iron: 1 mg   Sodium: 16 mg   Dietary Fiber: 2 gm

Creamy Carrot Soup

(Makes 4 servings)

Here's another dish that can be served hot or cold.

1 pound peeled and thinly sliced carrots
1 cup carrot juice (canned or fresh)
1 teaspoon vegan margarine
2 teaspoons orange juice concentrate
1 teaspoon curry powder
2 cups carrot juice
1 teaspoon lemon zest
1 cup silken tofu

In a large pot, simmer carrots, carrot juice, margarine, concentrate, and curry powder until almost all the liquid has evaporated, approximately 45 minutes.

In a blender or food processor, purée cooked carrots, carrot juice, lemon zest, and tofu and process until very smooth. Refrigerate soup for at least 2 hours or freeze until ready to eat.

Note: Serve this cold soup on a hot night or heat it and serve it hot on a cold night!

Total Calories Per Serving: 135   Total Fat as % of Daily Value: 5%
Protein: 5 gm   Fat: 3 gm   Carbohydrates: 23 gm   Calcium: 102 mg
Iron: 1 mg   Sodium: 146 mg   Dietary Fiber: 4 gm

Make Now, Use for the Week

The following recipes are not for freezing, but for refrigerating. Most will last for 5 days, if stored in airtight containers in a properly functioning refrigerator (USDA guidelines suggest that home refrigerators be kept at temperatures between 38 and 41 degrees Fahrenheit). Use the dressings for vegetable, pasta, bean, or tofu salads, instead of some of the mayonnaise called for in recipes. These dressings can also be used as a dip for veggies and chips or as marinades for grilling or roasting. For example, if you have some zucchini, mushrooms, tomatoes, seitan, or tofu you want to roast or grill, allow them to marinate in the Tomato-Mustard Vinaigrette, the Garlicky Caesar, or the Orange and Tahini Dressing. We even like some of these dressings on sliced fresh pineapple, sliced melon, apples, pears, and grapes.

A recipe for Cucumber Raita appears in Chapter 4. It, too, can be used as a salad dressing or tossed with pasta, rice, or couscous and a small amount of curry powder to make a curried salad. Raita can be combined with mashed avocado to make a cold summer soup or mixed with salsa to make a cold, creamy, spicy tomato soup. If you don't have the time or the inclination to prepare dressings, then select two or three commercial dressings and keep them in your refrigerator, so you have some flavor variety.

Once again, do not freeze any of the following recipes, but do refrigerate them. If you have any unused portions left at the end of 5 days (and this is the max!) discard them and prepare half a recipe the next time.

Peanut and Onion Dressing
(Makes approximately 1 pint or 16 servings)

This recipe has Thai influences and can be served cold as a dressing, or heated as a hot "cream" of peanut soup.

1 Tablespoon vegan margarine
1/4 cup finely chopped onion
2 Tablespoons finely chopped celery
2 Tablespoons flour
1-1/2 cups vegetable broth
3/4 cup (or 6 ounces) creamy peanut butter (don't use chunky style or freshly ground peanut butter, as the texture will not be correct)
1/2 cup silken tofu

Melt margarine in a large heavy frying pan over medium heat. Add onions and celery and sauté until tender, approximately 5 minutes. Add flour and stir to form a paste. Add broth and bring to a quick boil, stirring. Reduce heat and simmer until thickened, approximately 20 minutes. Mix in peanut butter and tofu, stirring vigorously. For a very creamy texture, pour into a blender and purée until very smooth. Allow dressing to cool before refrigerating.

Total Calories Per Serving: 88   Total Fat as % of Daily Value: 11%
Protein: 4 gm   Fat: 7 gm   Carbohydrates: 4 gm   Calcium: 8 mg
Iron: <1 mg   Sodium: 159 mg   Dietary Fiber: 1 gm

Tomato-Mustard Vinaigrette
(Makes approximately 1 cup or 8 servings)

This recipe is very South-of-France.

1 teaspoon prepared mustard
2 minced garlic cloves or 1 Tablespoon granulated
**   garlic**
1/4 cup red vinegar
2 Tablespoons lemon juice
1 Tablespoon oil (olive oil works well, but other oils are
**   fine)**
1 ounce or 2 Tablespoons tomato juice or vegetable
**   cocktail (such as V8)**
1/2 teaspoon soy sauce
1/4 teaspoon black pepper

Combine all the ingredients in a nonreactive bowl and whisk until well combined or place in a blender and process until well combined. Refrigerate until ready to use.

Total Calories Per Serving Using Olive Oil: 21
Total Fat as % of Daily Value: 3%
Protein: <1 gm   Fat: 2 gm   Carbohydrates: 2 gm   Calcium: 3 mg
Iron: <1 mg   Sodium: 43 mg   Dietary Fiber: <1 gm

Garlicky Caesar Dressing
(Makes 1/2 cup)

This will wake up green, pasta, and rice salads, as well as cooked veggies.

6 peeled garlic cloves (we told you it was garlicky!)
1 teaspoon olive oil (or other oil)
1 teaspoon red wine or balsamic vinegar
2 Tablespoons lemon juice
1 teaspoon water
1/2 teaspoon dry mustard (not prepared mustard)
1/4 teaspoon hot sauce or Tabasco sauce

In a small bowl, mash garlic and oil together to form a paste. Add remaining ingredients and whisk to combine. Refrigerate until ready to use.

Total Calories Per 2 Tablespoon Serving: 22
Total Fat as % of Daily Value: 2%
Protein: <1 gm   Fat: 1 gm   Carbohydrates: 2 gm   Calcium: 10 mg
Iron: <1 mg   Sodium: 3 mg   Dietary Fiber: <1 gm

Green and Creamy Dressing
(Makes 1 cup)

This is a dream as a salad dressing or a sandwich filling.

3/4 cup or 6 ounces silken tofu
1/4 cup soymilk
2 minced garlic cloves
1/4 cup minced parsley or cilantro
1 teaspoon dried oregano
1/2 teaspoon black pepper

Put all the ingredients in a blender and process until smooth.
Refrigerate until ready to use.

Total Calories Per Recipe: 136   Total Fat as % of Daily Value: 9%
Protein: 11 gm   Fat: 6 gm   Carbohydrates: 11 gm   Calcium: 114 mg
Iron: 4 mg   Sodium: 26 mg   Dietary Fiber: 3 gm

Orange Tahini Dressing

(Makes 1 cup)

Cook up the falafel! The tahini is coming!

1 Tablespoon tahini (sesame seed paste)
1 Tablespoon lemon juice
2 Tablespoons red vinegar or balsamic vinegar
1/2 cup water
1/2 cup peeled and chopped fresh orange
1/2 teaspoon dry mustard
2 teaspoon orange juice concentrate
1/4 teaspoon red pepper flakes

Put all the ingredients in a blender and process until smooth. Refrigerate until ready to use.

Total Calories Per Recipe: 168   Total Fat as % of Daily Value: 14%
Protein: 4 gm   Fat: 9 gm   Carbohydrates: 20 gm   Calcium: 69 mg
Iron: 2 mg   Sodium: 4 mg   Dietary Fiber: 4 gm

Low Fat Raspberry Marinade
(Makes 1 cup)

The taste is so large, you'll never guess this is lowfat.

2 teaspoon prepared mustard
2 Tablespoons mashed fresh or thawed, frozen
  raspberries
1 minced garlic clove
2 Tablespoons minced onion
1/2 cup vinegar (raspberry vinegar would be nice)
1/2 cup water
2 teaspoon lemon juice
2 teaspoons minced fresh parsley

In a medium-sized bowl, whisk all the ingredients together until well combined. Refrigerate until ready to use.

Total Calories Per Recipe: 77   Total Fat as % of Daily Value: 2%
Protein: 1 gm   Fat: 1 gm   Carbohydrates: 20 gm   Calcium: 40 mg
Iron: 1 mg   Sodium: 256 mg   Dietary Fiber: 2 gm

Roasted Garlic and Basil Spread
(Makes approximately 1 cup or 16 servings)

While we're on a garlic roll, we thought we'd add this garlic spread which can be used on salads. It can be mixed with some tofu or mayonnaise to thin it out and used as a marinade or used as a spread for sandwiches or a dip. There's some elbow grease involved, but it's worth it!

2 whole heads of garlic
2 teaspoons olive oil
1 cup fresh basil
1 teaspoon salt
1 teaspoon lemon juice

Preheat oven to 375 degrees. Rub unpeeled whole garlic heads with oil and wrap in foil. Bake at 375 degrees until garlic is very tender (easily pierced with a knife), approximately 30 minutes. Allow garlic to cool.

When cool, squeeze garlic pulp from heads into a small bowl. Using a potato masher or a strong fork and a bowl, mash the basil with the salt until it is a paste. Slowly add garlic and lemon and continue to mash until a combined paste is formed. Refrigerate spread until ready to use.

Total Calories Per Serving: 18   Total Fat as % of Daily Value: 1%
Protein: 1 gm   Fat: 1 gm   Carbohydrates: 3 gm   Calcium: 20 mg
Iron: <1 mg   Sodium: 147 mg   Dietary Fiber: <1 gm

Peperonata
(Makes 4 servings)

This is a traditional Italian specialty, which can be eaten hot or cold, used as a condiment (instead of salsa or sauce), served over pasta, rice, or cooked grains, or even stuffed into a pita or rolled into a tortilla.

2 Tablespoons olive oil
1 cup onions, cut into thin rings
1 minced garlic clove
1 cup chopped fresh tomatoes
3/4 cup green bell peppers, cut into strips
1/2 cup red bell peppers, cut into strips
2 cups cubed eggplant (not peeled)
1 teaspoon black pepper
1/8 teaspoon nutmeg

Heat a large frying pan and add oil. Add onions and garlic and sauté until onions are translucent, approximately 5 minutes. Add tomatoes, peppers, and eggplant. Cook, stirring, until almost all the liquid is evaporated. Add black pepper and nutmeg. Cool and refrigerate.

Total Calories Per Serving: 106   Total Fat as % of Daily Value: 11%
Protein: 2 gm   Fat: 7 gm   Carbohydrates: 11 gm   Calcium: 19 mg
Iron: 1 mg   Sodium: 7 mg   Dietary Fiber: 3 gm

Pepper Blast
(Makes 1 cup)

This adaptation of Rhodesian piri-piri is a fiery complement to tofu, tempeh, or grilled or steamed vegetables. Use, sparingly, as a condiment for dinnertime or brush it on tofu or veggies before you grill or roast them.

3 fresh or canned jalapeño chilies, seeded and chopped
2 fresh habañero chilies, seeded and chopped
2 Tablespoons lemon juice
2 Tablespoons fresh parsley, chopped
3/4 cup unsweetened canned coconut milk

In a small pan, combine chilies and lemon juice. Bring to a quick boil, reduce heat, cover, and simmer for 5 minutes. Add this mixture and fresh parsley to a blender canister and blend until smooth. Allow mixture to cool.

Add coconut milk to cooled mixture. Stir to blend. Refrigerate until ready to use.

Total Calories Per Recipe: 413   Total Fat as % of Daily Value: 57%
Protein: 7 gm   Fat: 37 gm   Carbohydrates: 23 gm   Calcium: 59 mg
Iron: 7 mg   Sodium: 39 mg   Dietary Fiber: 4 gm

Garlic Soup/Sauce
(Makes 1 pint)

Is this a sauce? Is this a robust soup? We can't decide, so serve it hot as a soup and cold as a sauce.

2 Tablespoons oil
3 garlic cloves peeled and thinly sliced
1 teaspoon dried thyme
1-1/2 cups vegetable broth
2 Tablespoons silken tofu
2 teaspoons white vinegar

Heat oil in a medium-sized frying pan. Add garlic and thyme and cook until garlic is translucent, approximately 5 minutes. Add broth, bring to a boil, and reduce heat to medium. Simmer until the liquid is reduced by a quarter and the garlic is very tender, about 15 minutes.

In a small bowl, whisk tofu and vinegar until creamy. Whisk mixture into the hot liquid and stir until thickened. Serve warm as soup or chill in the refrigerator and use as a sauce.

Total Calories Per Recipe: 303   Total Fat as % of Daily Value: 45%
Protein: 5gm   Fat: 29 gm   Carbohydrates: 9 gm   Calcium: 53 mg
Iron: 2 mg   Sodium: 1505 mg   Dietary Fiber: 1 gm

Ginger and Wine Marinated Fruit
(Makes 3 servings)

Serve this over vegan ice cream, sorbet, or apple, pear, or fresh peach slices.

4 cups diced mixed fruit (see note below)
3/4 cup water
3/4 cup vegan dry sweetener
1 cup dry white wine
2 teaspoons grated fresh ginger

Place fruit in a medium-sized plastic or glass container. Set aside.

In a small saucepan, cook water and sweetener over medium heat, stirring constantly, until sweetener dissolves. Bring to a boil and allow mixture to boil for 2 minutes. Reduce heat, add wine and ginger, and cook for 1 more minute, until heated thoroughly. Pour over fruit and combine. Cover and refrigerate until ready to use.

Note: Use combinations of soft and crunchy fruit, such as bananas, apples, and oranges or strawberries, blueberries, and pears. If no wine is available, you can use 3/4 cup apple juice mixed with 2 Tablespoons white vinegar.

Total Calories Per Serving Using Bananas, Apples, and Orange Sections: 369
Total Fat as % of Daily Value: 1%
Protein: 2 gm   Fat: 1 gm   Carbohydrates: 82 gm   Calcium: 51 mg
Iron: 1 mg   Sodium: 5 mg   Dietary Fiber: 5 gm

Hot Spicy Fruit Stew

(Makes 4 servings)

This can be a dessert on its own, paired with ice cream or sorbet, or used as a flavorful side dish for beans and grains.

1 cup applesauce
3/4 cup canned apricot halves, drained
3/4 cup canned pear halves, drained
1 cup canned peach halves, drained
1/2 cup canned pineapple tidbits, drained
1/3 cup vegan dry sweetener
1 teaspoon cinnamon
1 teaspoon ground ginger
1/2 teaspoon ground cloves
1/2 teaspoon ground nutmeg
2 Tablespoons vegan margarine

In a 1-quart oven or microwave dish layer half of the fruit. Top with half the amount of sweetener, cinnamon, ginger, cloves, and nutmeg and dot with half the amount of margarine. Repeat with remaining ingredients. Cover and microwave on high for 5 minutes, or until heated through, or bake at 375 degrees for 12-15 minutes or until heated through. Serve warm as a side dish or chill and serve over sorbet or vegan ice cream.

Total Calories Per Serving: 221   Total Fat as % of Daily Value: 9%
Protein: 1 gm   Fat: 6 gm   Carbohydrates: 44 gm   Calcium: 30 mg
Iron: 1 mg   Sodium: 80 mg   Dietary Fiber: 4 gm

Chapter Six

Grab-and-Go

This chapter has more ideas than recipes. When we think of grab-and-go, we think of meals that can be quickly assembled or prepared the night before, or both. The recipes we have included fall into one of two categories. They can be prepared and packaged in 5 minutes or less (if you're organized and do your chopping, measuring, etc. ahead of time), or they can be assembled and left to cook while you are getting ready to go.

The beverages in this chapter are easily transportable. Most of the smoothies can be part or all of a quick meal, and the hot beverages will do well in a thermos. If all you have time for is gulping a meal, be sure to toss several pieces of fruit, bagged nuts or seeds, bagged cold cereal or granola, dried fruit, or nut butter and crackers in your knapsack/briefcase.

Speaking of your knapsack/briefcase, be sure you have a good supply of containers and hot/cold transporting equipment. A thermos, insulated bags, cold packs, and mini insulated chests are necessary to keep foods and beverages at safe temperatures and to keep up the quality of your personal feast. Part of your daily ritual should be the cleaning and sanitizing of used food and beverage containers.

Grab-and-go is all about planning and timing. I like the pattern used by many of the families I stayed with while teaching above the Arctic Circle in Norway. Breakfast was a mini-smorgasbord of sliced cheeses, cucumbers, olives, onions, tomatoes, sliced boiled potatoes, sliced seasonal fruit, vegetable salads, and breads. There were waxed paper and paper bags on the table. When you finished your breakfast, you packed a lunch from the breakfast ingredients. If you were in a real hurry, you ate breakfast with one hand and assembled lunch with the other.

It sounds like a lot of ingredients, but almost everything had a shelf life of several days and only small amounts were prepared.

For example, if you sliced one tomato, one cucumber, a carrot or two, several pickles, and a small onion, and had a small package of sliced soy cheese, some canned sliced beets, and several boiled potatoes, they probably would only last through two or so breakfasts and several lunches. This created very little work, lots of nutrition, and lots of meals. By the way, the Norwegians thought the American tradition of eating sweets at breakfast was really weird. In Norway, sweets are reserved for the evening dessert and are usually some form of crepe served with fruit preserves. Cold cereal is very rare and Pop-Tarts are non-existent (thank goodness).

Keep an inventory of leftovers; they make great grab-and-go combinations. Here are some of our quick leftover creations:

- Toss leftover cooked pasta, especially vegan-filled pasta such as ravioli, gnocchi, and tortellini (see glossary), with rinsed, canned artichoke hearts, sliced olives, and sliced mushrooms. Use leftover pasta sauce or Italian salad dressing as a seasoning. This can be eaten hot or cold.

- Veggie-Bean sandwiches can be made with leftover cooked beans that have been mashed with mustard or vegan mayonnaise (or both). If you have them, you can add chopped onions, bell peppers or pimientos, celery, and shredded fresh basil or oregano. Spread the mixture on the bread, wrap, or roll of your choice and add Romaine lettuce or spinach (more nutrients than iceberg lettuce), shredded carrots, sliced cucumbers, or chopped tomatoes.

- Spicy tofu sandwiches can be made with mashed tofu (especially if you have a flavored tofu, such as smoked or barbecue) mixed with curry powder and a little vegan mayonnaise. Again, add what you have on hand, such as chopped onions, minced garlic, chopped celery, chopped bell peppers or chilies, chopped green or red grapes, etc. Stuff into a pita or roll into a tortilla.

114

- Check out those cup-of-noodles products. We're not recommending these as an every day lunch, but they can fit the bill on occasion. Read labels. Some of these "cup" products can be deceptively high in fat and salt. Bring along add-ins, such as leftover cooked, chopped veggies; nuts; shredded carrots and chopped onions; or canned beans to amp up both the nutrition and the interest. If you like, keep a baggie or a jar of nutritional yeast at your desk or in your knapsack to sprinkle over your creation.

- For a fast dessert or snack, mix chopped fresh and canned fruit, such as sliced strawberries and peaches, into mashed tofu. Sprinkle with a sweetener and cinnamon. This actually develops more flavor in the refrigerator, so prepare it the night before.

- Chapter 5 listed lots of frozen pizza ideas. Pop one in the oven the night before, then refrigerate it overnight. That's lunch the next day. Or pop one in the oven when you get up in the morning and treat yourself to a hot breakfast.

- Just about anything can be wrapped in a burrito or tucked into a pita. Nut butters with chopped nuts; salsa and chopped tofu; fake meat and chopped veggies; chopped veggies and hummus; leftover bean or potato dishes; soy cheese and shredded veggies.... The list goes on and on!

Check out the prepared foods offered by your local markets. Vegan options may include pasta salad or veggie salads tossed with Italian dressing or oil and vinegar; cooked rice salads (usually not made with mayonnaise); bean salads; hummus; salsa; carrot and celery sticks; cherry tomatoes; olives; pickles; radishes; vegan croutons; sliced cucumbers; sprouts; vegan chow mein noodles (crispy noodles); cut melon; pineapple chunks; grapes; and roasted peppers, to name some of the selections we've seen.

Beverages can be refreshing, stimulating, comforting, or a meal-in-a-glass, depending upon your schedule and your needs.

Fluid is an important part of your daily intake. Water, sparkling water, vegan milks (soy, rice, etc.), fruit and vegetable juices, decaffeinated coffee and teas, coffee substitutes, such as chicory and beet root, herb teas, fresh fruits and vegetables, and foods made largely from fluids, such as hot cereals and soups, are good sources of fluid. Caffeine and alcohol deplete the body of fluid. Remember when you indulge in caffeine and alcohol, you need to replace the fluid you'll lose. Check out the cold beverage recipes in this chapter. They'll make taking in sufficient fluids every day a snap.

To make some of the following recipes, you will need this equipment: blender, coffee maker, something in which to brew tea, assorted mixing bowls, and a pitcher or two. If you want to take these on the road with you, then you'll need an insulated mug (or a mini ice chest, or whatever you haul your meals in).

In your pantry you might stock coffee (instant or roasted and ground) or instant coffee; black or green tea; flavored or herbal teas; ground cinnamon; ground ginger; orange and lemon zest (unless you always have fresh oranges and lemons around); dried mint (unless you have fresh mint); vanilla extract; sweeteners of choice; and cocoa powder. We have a personal preference for decaffeinated tea and coffee, but you know what gets your engine going.

In your refrigerator/freezer, you might include plain soy or rice milk; chocolate-flavored soy, almond, or rice milk; ice cubes; orange or apple juice concentrate; frozen soy or rice ice cream; fresh fruit, such as bananas, melons, grapes, peaches, apricots, and fresh berries (in season); or frozen peaches and berries and/or canned peaches, pineapples, apricots, and blueberries. The fruit selection is up to you; these are just suggestions.

If you don't want to stock many different flavors of soy, rice, or almond milk, just have vanilla extract and chocolate syrup around to make vanilla or chocolate milk. In fact, if you keep milk, seltzer (sparkling water), and various extracts and syrups around, you can whip up refreshing or comforting hot or cold beverages whenever you want. For example, vanilla milk with orange extract and some orange juice concentrate; chocolate milk with butterscotch or caramel syrup; or vanilla milk with strawberry syrup make great, fast drinks. Try one of our personal favorites, a vegan egg cream (which contains neither eggs nor cream). In a glass, mix a small amount of non-dairy milk and chocolate syrup (in a medium drinking glass, approximately 2 inches of this combination should do it). Pour cold seltzer over the syrup, stir, and you've got a real, live, New York-style egg cream.

Enjoy the following grab-and-go recipes.

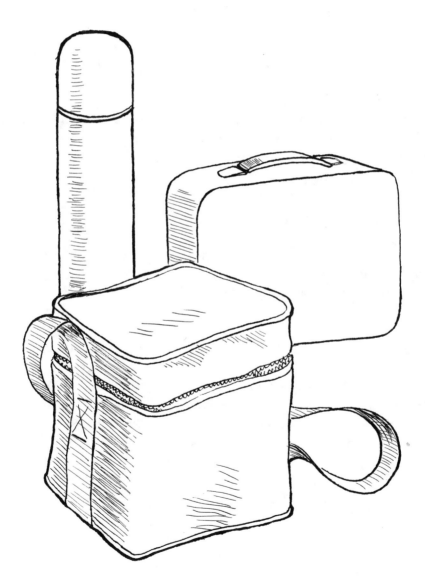

ENTRÉES

Green and Crunchy Salad
(Makes 2 servings)

Eat this as an entrée for lunch, then use the extras for a side dish at dinner. Extras could also be tossed into a container or bag to take on the road.

One (approximately 12-ounce) bag ready-to-use green salad or 2 cups tossed salad greens
1/4 cup chopped carrots
1/4 cup chopped red cabbage
1/4 cup chopped fresh mushrooms
1/2 cup chopped walnuts

Dry salad greens in a salad spinner, or by patting them with paper towels. Place greens in a large storage container (why mess up more bowls?) and toss all the ingredients together. Store in the refrigerator until ready to eat.

Note: When we need to save time, we purchase shredded carrots, shredded red cabbage, and sliced mushrooms. Look for them in the produce section of your local supermarket. You can use the extras to toss into other salads, or throw into soups or stir-fries. This salad can be eaten as is or served with your favorite salad dressing (we enjoy raspberry vinaigrette).

Total Calories Per Serving: 233   Total Fat as % of Daily Value: 29%
Protein: 8 gm   Fat: 19 gm   Carbohydrates: 13 gm   Calcium: 130 mg
Iron: 3 mg   Sodium: 52 mg   Dietary Fiber: 5 gm

Spur of the Moment Salad
(Makes 2 servings)

A great way to use extra bread, and a really simple preparation.

2 old pita bread or 2 slices stale whole wheat bread
1/2 cup cubed ripe tomato
1/4 cup peeled and cubed cucumber
1/8 cup diced red onion
2 Tablespoons sliced black olives
2 Tablespoons chopped fresh parsley or cilantro
1 teaspoon dried mint (or same amount finely chopped
**   fresh mint, if you've got it)**
1 Tablespoon olive oil (other oils are okay)
2 teaspoons balsamic or red wine vinegar
1/2 teaspoon black pepper

Rip bread into 1-inch pieces and set aside. In a medium-sized bowl, mix together tomato, cucumber, onion, olives, parsley or cilantro, and mint. In a small bowl, whisk olive oil and vinegar until well combined. Right before you are ready to eat, add the bread to the salad and toss with the dressing and pepper. If you are packing this as a lunch, pack the salad and the dressing separately. Mix together when ready to eat.

Total Calories Per Serving Using Pita Bread and Cilantro: 260
Total Fat as % of Daily Value: 15%
Protein: 7 gm   Fat: 10 gm   Carbohydrates: 40 gm   Calcium: 29 mg
Iron: 3 mg   Sodium: 420 mg   Dietary Fiber: 6 gm

Veggie Burger Grab
(Makes 1 serving)

Use up an extra veggie burger or veggie hot dog (the recipe works just as well with veggie hot dogs) from dinner. This recipe can be made the night before or prepared in the morning.

1 cooked veggie burger, diced
2 slices tomato, diced
1 slice onion, diced
2 teaspoons ketchup
1 teaspoon mustard
1/2 cup Romaine lettuce, shredded
3 slices pickle
1 tortilla or pita bread

In a microwave-safe bowl, combine veggie burger, tomato, onion, ketchup, and mustard. Heat on high for 2 minutes or until warmed through.

Place lettuce and pickles on a tortilla or pita. Spread veggie burger mixture on top of the lettuce. Roll tightly and eat right away or pack for a portable meal.

Note: If no microwave is available, you can preheat the oven to 400 degrees, wrap the mixture in foil, and bake for approximately 7 minutes.

Total Calories Per Serving Using Pita Bread: 471
Total Fat as % of Daily Value: 4%
Protein: 17 gm   Fat: 3 gm   Carbohydrates: 99 gm   Calcium: 341 mg
Iron: 3 mg   Sodium: 1003 mg   Dietary Fiber: 18 gm

Variations:

- <u>Mediterranean Grab</u>: instead of ketchup, mustard, and pickle, use 2 Tablespoons pizza or spaghetti sauce and 1 Tablespoon sliced olives

- <u>Southwestern Grab</u>: instead of ketchup, mustard, and pickle, use 2 Tablespoons salsa, 1 teaspoon chopped chilies or bell peppers, and 1/4 teaspoon hot sauce

- <u>Middle Eastern Grab</u>: instead of ketchup, mustard, and pickle, use 2 Tablespoons hummus, 1 teaspoon vegan mayonnaise, 1 teaspoon sliced green olives, and 1/2 teaspoon paprika

- <u>Barbecue Grab</u>: instead of ketchup, use 2 teaspoons barbecue sauce (the rest of the ingredients stay the same)

- <u>Curried Grab</u>: instead of ketchup, use 2 teaspoons vegan mayonnaise (the rest of the ingredients stay the same) and add 1 teaspoon curry powder

Speedy Tostadas
(Makes 2 servings)

Use taco shells, tortillas, or even pitas for this recipe.

3/4 cup veggie chili (canned or leftover)
2 vegan taco shells
1/3 cup shredded lettuce
1/4 cup chopped bell peppers
1/4 cup salsa
2 Tablespoons vegan sour cream or shredded soy
    cheese, if desired

Warm chili on a stove or in a microwave until heated through.
Divide chili in half and place in taco shells. Top with lettuce,
peppers, salsa, and vegan sour cream or shredded cheese.

Total Calories Per Serving Using Soy Cheese: 185
Total Fat as % of Daily Value: 8%
Protein: 16 gm   Fat: 5 gm   Carbohydrates: 23 gm   Calcium: 98 mg
Iron: 4 mg   Sodium: 528 mg   Dietary Fiber: 5 gm

Lemon Tofu and Spinach Bake

(Makes 3 servings)

Assemble this the night before and bake it in the morning while you are getting ready to go. Remember, you need thawed spinach, so let it thaw one day ahead in the refrigerator, or thaw it in a microwave right before you're ready to use it.

1-1/4 cups thawed, frozen spinach, drained
1/4 cup chopped onions
2 Tablespoons lemon juice
1 cup crumbled firm tofu
2 teaspoons granulated garlic
1/2 teaspoon red pepper flakes
1 cup crushed tortilla chips

Preheat oven to 375 degrees. In a medium-sized bowl, combine all ingredients, except chips, and mix well.

Place a thin layer of chips in individual baking dishes. Cover with spinach mixture and top with remaining chips. Bake at 375 degrees for 15 minutes or until set.

Total Calories Per Serving: 246   Total Fat as % of Daily Value: 19%
Protein: 17 gm   Fat: 13 gm   Carbohydrates: 22 gm   Calcium: 244 mg
Iron: 11 mg   Sodium: 161 mg   Dietary Fiber: 6 gm

Baked Beans Quesadillas
(Makes 3 whole quesadillas)

If you don't have the vegan cheese, a possible substitute would be mashed tofu.

Vegetable oil spray
3 six-inch vegan corn tortillas, cut in half
1 cup canned baked beans
1 cup shredded vegan cheese
3 Tablespoons chopped fresh cilantro or parsley
For garnish, as desired: chopped fresh or canned tomatoes, drained; chopped or sliced chilies or green bell peppers; additional shredded vegan cheese; and/or sliced black olives

Place 3 tortilla halves on a clean work surface. Spray one side with oil. Turn sprayed side down. Place 1/3 cup beans in the center of three of the tortilla halves. Top beans with vegan cheese and cilantro. Cover with remaining tortilla halves. Spray tops with oil.

Cooking options:
1. On barbecue, grill on each side until golden brown and crisp.
2. Spray a large frying pan with oil and cook on each side for three minutes, or until each side is golden.
3. The following works well when you're getting ready in the morning. Preheat oven to 400 degrees. Spray baking sheet with oil. Place quesadillas on sheet and bake (no need to turn) for 8-10 minutes or until golden.

Serve with garnish, as desired.

Note: Canned baked beans with barbecue flavor or the addition of 2 Tablespoons of barbecue sauce mixed into the beans adds to the flavor.

Total Calories Per Quesadilla Using Cilantro (minus garnish): 150
Total Fat as % of Daily Value: 3%
Protein: 7 gm   Fat: 2 gm   Carbohydrates: 30 gm   Calcium: 135 mg
Iron: 1 mg   Sodium: 339 mg   Dietary Fiber: 6 gm

Oktoberfest Kraut and Beans
(Makes 2 servings)

This is another recipe to make the night before and let cook the next morning while you're getting ready. If you have leftover pasta or rice, pack it as an accompaniment.

1-1/2 cups canned or fresh sauerkraut
1-1/2 cups canned baked beans
1/4 cup water
2 teaspoons prepared mustard
1 teaspoon caraway seeds

Preheat oven to 400 degrees. Place sauerkraut in strainer or colander. Rinse with cold water and allow sauerkraut to drain. In a medium-sized baking dish, combine sauerkraut, beans, water, mustard, and caraway seeds. Mix well. Bake at 400 degrees for 10-12 minutes or until thoroughly heated.

Total Calories Per Serving: 206   Total Fat as % of Daily Value: 3%
Protein: 10 gm   Fat: 2 gm   Carbohydrates: 44 gm   Calcium: 141 mg
Iron: 1 mg   Sodium: 1465 mg   Dietary Fiber: 13 gm

Garbanzo-Spinach Curry
(Makes 2 servings)

This recipe can be eaten hot or cold on its own, with rice or cooked grains, or even rolled into a tortilla or a pita.

1 cup thawed, frozen chopped spinach
1/2 cup canned chopped tomatoes (not drained)
1 cup canned or cooked garbanzo beans, drained
1 Tablespoon granulated garlic
3 teaspoons curry powder
Garnish (if desired): 1/4 cup unsweetened grated or
    flaked coconut

In a medium-sized saucepan, combine all the ingredients except coconut. Bring to a fast boil, reduce heat, and cover. Allow mixture to simmer for 10 minutes or until heated thoroughly. Garnish with coconut.

Total Calories Per Serving (minus coconut): 196
Total Fat as % of Daily Value: 3%
Protein: 10 gm   Fat: 2 gm   Carbohydrates: 38 gm   Calcium: 164 mg
Iron: 5 mg   Sodium: 508 mg   Dietary Fiber: 10gm

One Dish Potato Bar
(Makes 1 serving)

This is really a leftover dish. Prepare one or two extra baked potatoes the next time you are having them for dinner.

1 baked potato
1/4 cup cooked beans
2 teaspoons salsa or pizza sauce
1 teaspoon chopped onions
1 teaspoon chopped bell peppers
1 Tablespoon canned or thawed frozen cut corn

Cut potato in half, lengthwise. Scoop out potato, being sure to keep the shells intact.

In a small bowl, mix and mash together the beans, salsa or sauce, onions, peppers, and corn. Fill potato shells. Microwave on high for 3 minutes or until hot, or cover and bake at 400 degrees for 7 minutes or until hot.

Total Calories Per Serving Using Red Kidney Beans and Salsa: 221
Total Fat as % of Daily Value: 1%
Protein: 8 gm   Fat: 1 gm   Carbohydrates: 48 gm   Calcium: 19 mg
Iron: 2 mg   Sodium: 38 mg   Dietary Fiber: 9 gm

HOT BEVERAGES

Almond Latte

(Makes 1 serving)

Capture the flavor of almonds and coffee in this drink.

1 cup brewed coffee
2/3 cup almond milk (or soy or rice milk with 1/4
   teaspoon almond extract added)
1 Tablespoon vegan dry sweetener
1/2 teaspoon almond extract
1 teaspoon maple syrup
1 teaspoon chopped almonds, if desired

Combine coffee, milk, sweetener, extract, and syrup. Mix well.
For a hot beverage, heat the ingredients in a microwave or on
the stove; for a cold beverage pour mixture over ice or freeze for
an almond/coffee slush. Top with almonds.

Total Calories Per Serving: 153   Total Fat as % of Daily Value: 6%
Protein: 5 gm   Fat: 4 gm   Carbohydrates: 21 gm   Calcium: 21 mg
Iron: 1 mg   Sodium: 25 mg   Dietary Fiber: 2 gm

Peppermint Chocolate Latte
(Makes 1 serving)

The mint adds "cool" to this recipe.

1 cup brewed coffee
1 Tablespoon unsweetened cocoa powder
1/4 teaspoon peppermint extract (or 2 peppermint
    hard candies melted in 1/4 cup boiling water)
1/2 cup chocolate soy, rice, or almond milk
2 teaspoons vegan dry sweetener, if desired

Mix together coffee, cocoa, and peppermint. Heat milk on a stove or in a microwave until steamy. Pour milk into coffee mixture and stir. Drink while hot, or pour over ice for a cold beverage.

Note: If you have any hanging around, a candy cane or peppermint stick makes a nice swizzle stick.

Total Calories Per Serving Using Soymilk: 144
Total Fat as % of Daily Value: 4%
Protein: 4 gm   Fat: 3 gm   Carbohydrates: 24 gm   Calcium: 42 mg
Iron: 2 mg   Sodium: 58 mg   Dietary Fiber: 3 gm

Orange Chocolate Latte
(Makes 1 serving)

This tastes just like a chocolate-covered orange!

1 cup brewed coffee
1 Tablespoon chocolate syrup
1 teaspoon fresh or dried orange zest
1 teaspoon orange juice concentrate
2/3 cup chocolate soy, rice, or almond milk

Combine coffee, syrup, zest, and orange juice concentrate. Heat chocolate milk on a stove or in a microwave until steamy. Combine milk with coffee mixture and stir. Drink while hot, or pour over ice for a cold beverage.

Total Calories Per Serving Using Soymilk: 206
Total Fat as % of Daily Value: 6%
Protein: 6 gm   Fat: 4 gm   Carbohydrates: 37 gm   Calcium: 53 mg
Iron: 1 mg   Sodium: 120 mg   Dietary Fiber: 1 gm

Lemonade Tea
(Makes 1 serving)

This is a refreshing, rejuvenating combination.

1 cup brewed green or herbal tea
2 Tablespoons lemon juice
1 Tablespoon vegan dry sweetener
1/2 teaspoon lemon zest

Combine ingredients in a small pot or microwave-safe glass. Heat until bubbly. Drink hot, or pour over ice for a cold beverage.

Total Calories Per Serving: 56   Total Fat as % of Daily Value: <1%
Protein: <1 gm   Fat: <1 gm   Carbohydrates: 15 gm   Calcium: 4 mg
Iron: <1 mg   Sodium: <1 mg   Dietary Fiber: <1 gm

Citrus Fruit Tea

(Makes 1 serving)

There's more than one way to get your servings of citrus!

1 cup brewed black or green tea
1/4 teaspoon orange zest
1/4 teaspoon lemon zest
1 Tablespoon orange juice concentrate
2 teaspoons orange marmalade

Place tea in a small pot or microwave-safe glass. Mix all ingredients together, stir, and allow to heat until bubbly. Drink while hot.

Total Calories Per Serving: 62   Total Fat as % of Daily Value: <1%
Protein: <1 gm   Fat: <1 gm   Carbohydrates: 16 gm   Calcium: 12 mg
Iron: <1 mg   Sodium: 8 mg   Dietary Fiber: <1 gm

Gingery Tea

(Makes 1 serving)

This will calm your nerves and delight your taste buds.

1/8 cup sliced, peeled fresh ginger
1/4 teaspoon lemon zest
1 cup boiling water
2 teaspoons vegan dry sweetener, if desired

Place ginger and lemon in the bottom of a large cup or mug. Pour boiling water over ginger and allow to steep for 3 minutes. Remove ginger, sweeten if desired, and drink hot, or pour over ice for a cold beverage.

Total Calories Per Serving: 41   Total Fat as % of Daily Value: <1%
Protein: <1 gm   Fat: <1 gm   Carbohydrates: 10 gm   Calcium: 3 mg
Iron: <1 mg   Sodium: 2 mg   Dietary Fiber: <1 gm

Rainy Day Tea

(Makes 1 serving)

Chase the blues away with this beverage.

1 cup brewed black or green tea
1/4 teaspoon ground ginger
1/4 teaspoon cloves
1/8 teaspoon cinnamon
1/8 teaspoon orange zest
1 teaspoon vegan dry sweetener, if desired

Place tea in small pot or microwave-safe glass. Add remaining ingredients and heat until bubbly. Drink while hot, or refrigerate for a cold beverage.

Total Calories Per Serving: 20   Total Fat as % of Daily Value: <1%
Protein: <1 gm   Fat: <1 gm   Carbohydrates: 5 gm   Calcium: 8 mg
Iron: <1 mg   Sodium: 2 mg   Dietary Fiber: <1 gm

COLD BEVERAGES

Orange Swirl
(Makes 1 serving)

This is sunshine in a glass!

3/4 cup almond milk (or soy or rice milk with 1/4 teaspoon almond extract added)
1/2 cup orange sorbet
1/4 cup vanilla soy or rice ice cream
1 Tablespoon orange juice concentrate
1/4 cup canned, drained mandarin orange segments

Put all the ingredients, except mandarin oranges, in a blender canister. Cover and blend on high until smooth. Pour over ice and serve, or freeze for an orange slush. Garnish with mandarin oranges.

Note: This can be made with lemonade or limeade and lemon or lime sorbet.

Total Calories Per Serving Using Soymilk: 351
Total Fat as % of Daily Value: 14%
Protein: 7 gm   Fat: 9 gm   Carbohydrates: 62 gm   Calcium: 20 mg
Iron: 1 mg   Sodium: 148 mg   Dietary Fiber: 4 gm

Chocolate-Covered Cherry Smoothie
(Makes 1 serving)

Drink this as is or freeze it for a wonderful dessert or snack.

3/4 cup chocolate soy, rice, or almond milk (or plain or vanilla milk with 1 Tablespoon chocolate syrup)
1/2 cup thawed frozen cherries (be sure they're pitted!)
1 Tablespoon chocolate syrup
1/3 cup soy or rice vanilla ice cream
3 ice cubes
2 Tablespoons vegan chocolate chips, if desired

Combine all the ingredients except chocolate chips in a blender canister. Cover and blend on high until smooth. Garnish with chocolate chips.

Total Calories Per Serving Using Soymilk (minus chips): 449
Total Fat as % of Daily Value: 19%
Protein: 9 gm   Fat: 12 gm   Carbohydrates: 78 gm   Calcium: 64 mg
Iron: 1 mg   Sodium: 269 mg   Dietary Fiber: 3 gm

Raspberries and Cream Smoothie
(Makes 1 serving)

This is a real "smooth" smoothie. Use it as a beverage or a dessert.

3/4 cup vanilla soy, rice, or almond milk
3/4 cup thawed frozen raspberries
2 Tablespoons raspberry preserves
1/3 cup vanilla soy or rice ice cream

Combine all the ingredients in a blender canister. Cover and blend on high until smooth. Serve cold or freeze for a raspberry cream slush.

Note: If raspberries and/or raspberry preserves are not available, strawberries can be used.

Total Calories Per Serving Using Soymilk and Soy Ice Cream: 531
Total Fat as % of Daily Value: 15%
Protein: 7 gm   Fat: 10 gm   Carbohydrates: 106 gm   Calcium: 178 mg
Iron: 2 mg   Sodium: 228 mg   Dietary Fiber: 8 gm

Mint Chocolate
Peanut Butter Refresher
(Makes 2 servings)

An occasional indulgence is a good thing. If you want to leave out the liqueur, melt two mint candies in 2 Tablespoons water or use peppermint extract instead. This drink is not for children.

1-1/2 cups vanilla rice or soy ice cream
2 Tablespoons chocolate syrup
2 Tablespoons crème de menthe liqueur
1-1/2 Tablespoons peanut butter
Fresh mint leaves to garnish, if desired

Place ice cream, syrup, liqueur, and peanut butter in a blender canister. Cover and blend until very smooth. Pour into chilled glasses, garnish with mint leaves, and enjoy!

Total Calories Per Serving Using Soy Ice Cream: 470
Total Fat as % of Daily Value: 35%
Protein: 7 gm   Fat: 23 gm   Carbohydrates: 51 gm   Calcium: 8 mg
Iron: 1 mg   Sodium: 381 mg   Dietary Fiber: 1 gm

Banana-Blueberry Smoothie
(Makes 2 servings)

This tastes like it should have a pie crust wrapped around it.

2 ripe bananas, sliced (about 2 cups)
1/2 cup vanilla soy or rice milk
1/2 cup fresh, or thawed frozen blueberries
1 Tablespoon apple juice concentrate

Place all the ingredients in a blender canister. Cover and blend until smooth. Place in freezer for 15 minutes before drinking, or allow it to freeze thoroughly for a frozen dessert.

Total Calories Per Serving Using Soymilk: 180
Total Fat as % of Daily Value: 2%
Protein: 3 gm   Fat: 2 gm   Carbohydrates: 42 gm   Calcium: 62 mg
Iron: 1 mg   Sodium: 26 mg   Dietary Fiber: 4 gm

Mongo Mango Smoothie
(Makes 2 servings)

Mango juice (or nectar) is available fresh, frozen, and canned. It tastes decadent and is packed with potassium and vitamin A.

1 cup mango juice
1/2 cup vanilla soy or rice milk
1/2 cup banana slices
1/2 teaspoon nutmeg

Place all the ingredients in a blender canister. Cover and blend until smooth. Place in freezer for 15 minutes before drinking or allow it to freeze thoroughly for a frozen dessert.

Total Calories Per Serving Using Soymilk: 149
Total Fat as % of Daily Value: 2%
Protein: 2 gm   Fat: 2 gm   Carbohydrates: 34 gm   Calcium: 59 mg
Iron: 2 mg   Sodium: 26 mg   Dietary Fiber: 2 gm

Pineapple Smoothie
(Makes 2 servings)

Enjoy this tropical fruit salad in a glass!

1/2 cup canned crushed pineapple, not drained
1 cup orange juice
1 medium banana, sliced
1 cup silken tofu

Place all the ingredients in a blender canister. Cover and blend until smooth. If you're not going to drink this immediately, it can be refrigerated, but will need to be stirred or reblended just prior to serving.

Note: To add some "fire" to this icy drink, blend in 2 teaspoons of fresh grated ginger.

Total Calories Per Serving: 198   Total Fat as % of Daily Value: 6%
Protein: 8 gm   Fat: 4 gm   Carbohydrates: 35 gm   Calcium: 64 mg
Iron: 2 mg   Sodium: 8 mg   Dietary Fiber: 2 gm

Watermelon Lemonade
(Makes 4 servings)

This drink is pink and pretty!

6 cups cubed and seeded watermelon
1/4 cup fresh or thawed frozen raspberries
1 cup water
1/2 cup vegan dry sweetener
1/2 cup fresh or frozen lemon juice

Place watermelon, raspberries, and water in a blender canister. Cover and blend until very smooth. Add sweetener and lemon juice; blend only until mixed. Pour into a nonreactive container and refrigerate until ready to drink. Stir before pouring.

Total Calories Per Serving: 181   Total Fat as % of Daily Value: 2%
Protein: 2 gm   Fat: 1 gm   Carbohydrates: 45 gm   Calcium: 22 mg
Iron: <1 mg   Sodium: 5 mg   Dietary Fiber: 2 gm

Gingered Lemon, Lime, or Orange-ade
(Makes 4 servings)

Enjoy sweet, spice, and tang all rolled into one glass.

1/4 cup peeled and chopped fresh ginger
2 cups boiling water
1/2 cup vegan dry sweetener
1 cup fresh lemon, lime, or orange juice
2 cups cold water

Place ginger into a large cup or glass and pour boiling water over it. Let mixture steep for 1 hour. Strain ginger, keeping liquid and discarding solids. Mix sweetener into liquid, and allow mixture to cool.

138

Combine ginger liquid, juice, and cold water. Stir and allow beverage to cool before drinking, or pour over ice.

Total Calories Per Serving Using Lemon Juice: 116
Total Fat as % of Daily Value: <1%
Protein: <1 gm   Fat: <1 gm   Carbohydrates: 31 gm   Calcium: 8 mg
Iron: <1 mg   Sodium: 5 mg   Dietary Fiber: <1 gm

Mango Lemonade
(Makes 4 servings)

Here you'll find vitamin A and potassium masquerading as a cool drink.

2 peeled and cubed ripe mangos or 2 cups thawed, frozen mango cubes
2 cups cold water
1 cup lemon juice
1/4 cup vegan dry sweetener (or sweeten to your taste)

Place mango in a blender canister. Cover and process until puréed. Pour into a pitcher. Add water, lemon juice, and sweetener; stir. Allow lemonade to cool before serving, or pour over ice.

Total Calories Per Serving: 131   Total Fat as % of Daily Value: <1%
Protein: 1 gm   Fat: <1 gm   Carbohydrates: 35 gm   Calcium: 15 mg
Iron: <1 mg   Sodium: 3 mg   Dietary Fiber: 2 gm

Chapter Seven

Desserts and Snacks

If you don't have time to prepare a dessert from scratch, shop and stock creatively. Orange sorbet with twists of orange peel, for example, served with chocolate or carob sauce (canned syrup) or orange marmalade can make you feel pampered and takes little time to toss together. Melon with frosted grapes (washed grapes rolled in a vegan dry sweetener while still damp and put in the freezer for approximately 15 minutes) is a quick dessert, as are slices of oranges or grapefruit sprinkled with raspberry preserves and fresh ginger.

Sorbet or soy or rice ice cream can be a basis for countless desserts. Open a can of peaches, plums, apricots, or pears, then add vegan ice cream, sprinkle on some granola, nuts, or cold cereal, and you've created a treat. Layer ice cream with fresh or thawed, frozen fruit to make a fast parfait. Throw vegan ice cream in a blender with bananas and berries, pour the mixture into prepared tart shells or a graham cracker crust, allow to freeze for about an hour, and there's an ice cream pie. Banana splits require only bananas, ice cream, maple syrup, nuts, and sliced fruit. Make your own frozen dessert by whipping soy yogurt with fruit or tofu, some sweetener, and fruit until smooth, then freeze until solid. Let your imagination fly! And don't forget that nutritional yeast goes well as part of an ice cream topping.

If you have a little more time, and especially if you have some fruit that's a little older than you'd like, think about fruit sautés. Peel and cut apples, pears, peaches, nectarines, apricots, or pineapple into thin wedges and quickly sauté with a small amount of margarine and dry sweetener. Add spices, such as cinnamon, nutmeg, orange or lemon zest, ginger, mace, or cloves and toss in dried fruit, such as apricots, raisins, or figs. Eat hot on its own or serve over sorbet or cake. This sauté will last at least 2 days in the refrigerator and can be added to hot cereal, reheated in the oven or the microwave, or mixed into granola.

Many people prefer to eat several small meals a day, rather than two or three large meals. Some health experts feel that five or six meals eaten throughout the day distribute energy and nutrients more efficiently. That's where snacks come in. Make them count! Combine nutritional value with fun foods. Pita, veggie chips, or veggie sticks with hummus or salsa, fruited granola, and mini-pizzas piled high with shredded veggies are all good examples of snacks that pack flavor, vitamins, and fun.

When you're stocking up for your day, be sure to include some snacks and beverages. Remember, you're dedicated to planning your healthy eating and treating yourself well. When you feel low on energy, you'll be able to reach into your knapsack or briefcase to recharge with some carrot-orange cookies, chili-popcorn, or a container of homemade cherry cobbler. Enjoy!

DESSERTS

Baked Pears in Apple Cider Syrup
(Makes 4 servings)

This is an elegant dessert. Serve it in stemmed glasses, garnished with some berries or fresh mint. Be sure to try a variety of pears.

4 firm-but-ripe pears
2 Tablespoons fresh lemon juice
2 cups apple cider
1/4 cup apple juice concentrate
1 teaspoon vanilla extract
1 cinnamon stick or 2 teaspoons ground cinnamon

Core, but do not peel pears. In a large pot, combine remaining ingredients. Bring to a boil and reduce heat. Allow to simmer for 5 minutes.

Add pears, keeping them upright. Allow to simmer until they are soft, about 15 minutes. Remove pears from liquid. Allow liquid to continue to cook until it is thick and syrupy, about 10 minutes. Serve pears and liquid warm or cold.

Note: You can use apples or fresh peaches in this recipe instead of pears.

Total Calories Per Serving: 147   Total Fat as % of Daily Value: 1%
Protein: 1 gm   Fat: 1 gm   Carbohydrates: 36 gm   Calcium: 32 mg
Iron: 1 mg   Sodium: 9 mg   Dietary Fiber: 5 gm

Pear Pie

(Makes one 9-inch pie, about 6 large slices)

Who says pie has to be apple?

6 ripe, but still firm Bartlett or Bosc pears, peeled, cored, and quartered
4 Tablespoons vegan dry sweetener
2 Tablespoons raisins
1 teaspoon vanilla extract
1 teaspoon lemon zest
1 Tablespoon cornstarch
9-inch frozen pie shell, not baked

Preheat oven to 400 degrees. In a large bowl, combine pears, sweetener, raisins, vanilla, and zest. Cover and set aside for 1 hour.

Place a colander in a large frying pan. Pour the pears into the colander and allow the juice to drip into the pan. Heat the pan with the juices, bring to a fast boil, reduce heat, and simmer until syrupy, about 3 minutes. If there isn't at least 3/4 cup of juice left, add some apple juice. Set aside.

Toss pears with cornstarch and mix until cornstarch is absorbed. Toss syrupy juice over pears and toss until mixed. Pour into a 9-inch pie shell. Cover with foil and bake at 400 degrees for 40 minutes or until juices are bubbling and fruit is tender.

Note: In season, fresh ripe plums can be used instead of pears.

Total Calories Per Serving: 255   Total Fat as % of Daily Value: 12%
Protein: 2 gm   Fat: 8 gm   Carbohydrates: 48 gm   Calcium: 25 mg
Iron: 1 mg   Sodium: 137 mg   Dietary Fiber: 4gm

Pears in Parchment
(Makes 4 servings)

This is an elegant dessert also known as oven-poached pears. Purée some raspberries or strawberries so you can serve the pears on a pink palette.

4 Tablespoons apricot or raspberry jam or preserves
4 ripe Bartlett or Bosc pears
4 Tablespoons chopped almonds or hazelnuts
4 teaspoons vegan margarine
4 teaspoons apple juice concentrate
2 teaspoons ground ginger
2 teaspoons lemon or orange zest

Preheat oven to 375 degrees. Measure the pears and cut four pieces of foil 2-1/2 times the size of the pears (you are going to be folding the pears into a foil envelope, so you need room).

Wash the pears and cut them almost half way through so that you create wedges still held together by the base of the pear.

Double (fold in half) each piece of foil. Place a Tablespoon of jam in the center of each folded piece of foil. Place one pear on top of the jam (it's okay if the wedges separate a bit). Sprinkle 1 Tablespoon nuts, 1 teaspoon margarine, 1 teaspoon apple juice concentrate, 1/2 teaspoon ground ginger, and 1/2 teaspoon zest on each pear. Be sure the pears are standing upright and then wrap them in a loose, but sealed, foil envelope. Place pears on a baking sheet or in a baking dish and bake for 10 minutes at 375 degrees or until the pears are soft and heated through.

Notes: The pears can be prepared the night before and stored in the refrigerator until ready to cook. Once cooked, do not store pears in foil; store in plastic or glass. You can use apples, fresh peaches, or nectarines in this recipe, instead of pears.

Total Calories Per Serving: 182   Total Fat as % of Daily Value: 11%
Protein: 2 gm   Fat: 7 gm   Carbohydrates: 30 gm   Calcium: 30 mg
Iron: <1 mg   Sodium: 54 mg   Dietary Fiber: 5 gm

Cool and Smooth Fruit

(Makes 1 serving)

This is a wonderful dessert sauce. Serve it over vegan ice cream, pudding, or fruit salad.

1 cup frozen melon or berries
2 teaspoons vegan dry sweetener
1/2 teaspoon dried mint
Soy ice cream or sorbet

Place fruit, sweetener, and mint in a blender and purée until very smooth. Pour over ice cream or sorbet and serve immediately.

Total Calories For Sauce Only: 92   Total Fat as % of Daily Value: <1%
Protein: 2 gm   Fat: <1 gm   Carbohydrates: 22 gm   Calcium: 29 mg
Iron: 2 mg   Sodium: 56 mg   Dietary Fiber: 1 gm

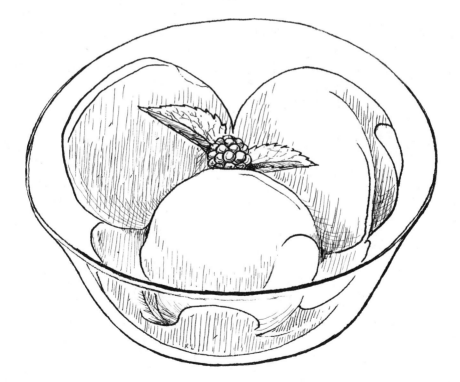

Chocolate Dream
(Makes one 9-inch pie, about 6 large slices)

Fast to whip up, this is a smooth, creamy, chocolate-lover's dream.

1/4 cup melted vegan margarine
1 cup vegan graham cracker crumbs
2 Tablespoons maple syrup
1-1/4 cups chocolate or carob chips
2-1/4 cups silken tofu
2 Tablespoons maple syrup

Preheat oven to 375 degrees. In a medium-sized bowl, mix margarine, crumbs, and 2 Tablespoons maple syrup. Press into a 9-inch pie tin and bake at 375 degrees for 5 minutes or until golden. Place pie crust in the refrigerator and allow to chill.

Melt chips in a medium-sized pot; stir for smooth consistency. Set aside when melted. In a blender, combine tofu and 2 Tablespoons maple syrup and blend until smooth. Add melted chips and blend until smooth. Pour into the pie crust. Refrigerate until firm, at least 45 minutes.

Total Calories Per Serving: 412   Total Fat as % of Daily Value: 31%
Protein: 7 gm   Fat: 20 gm   Carbohydrates: 52 gm   Calcium: 71 mg
Iron: 3 mg   Sodium: 226 mg   Dietary Fiber: 1 gm

Graham Pudding Parfaits

(Makes 3 parfaits)

These parfaits are a fast treat and a nice ending to the day.

1 cup vegan graham crackers, broken into small pieces
1 cup mixed berries (fresh or thawed, frozen)
1 small box (3.5 ounce) instant vegan pudding mix
1-1/2 cups rice or soymilk
3 Tablespoons shredded coconut

Place a thin layer of graham crackers in the bottom of three parfait cups or small bowls. Place a thin layer of berries on top. Prepare pudding according to package directions. Complete parfaits by layering pudding, graham crackers, and berries until all ingredients are used. Garnish with coconut and chill for 1 hour before serving.

Note: This dessert can be frozen as well. In addition to berries, use sliced bananas and peaches. Fruit-flavored soy yogurt can be used instead of pudding and milk, if desired.

Total Calories Per Serving: 371   Total Fat as % of Daily Value: 13%
Protein: 7 gm   Fat: 8 gm   Carbohydrates: 70 gm   Calcium: 27 mg
Iron: 3 mg   Sodium: 734 mg   Dietary Fiber: 5 gm

Fruit and Graham Crisp
(Makes 3 servings)

This dessert is tops in comfort food!

1 cup canned sliced peaches, drained
2 Tablespoons raisins, dried cranberries, or dried
  cherries
1/2 teaspoon cinnamon
1/2 cup vegan graham crackers, broken into small
  pieces
1/4 teaspoon cinnamon
1/4 teaspoon ground ginger
2 teaspoons melted vegan margarine
Sorbet or soy ice cream, if desired

Preheat oven to 350 degrees. In a 9-inch pie pan combine peaches, raisins, and cinnamon. Bake for 10 minutes.

In a small bowl, combine graham crackers, cinnamon, ginger, and margarine until mixed. Spoon coating over fruit. Bake at 350 degrees for 10 minutes or until thoroughly heated. Serve warm, topped with sorbet or soy ice cream, if desired. You can also allow the crisp to chill before serving.

Note: This is a good way to use leftover fruit. Combine several kinds of canned fruit, such as pineapple and pears, and add ripe, cut fruit, such as peaches, apricots, or berries.

Total Calories Per Serving (minus sorbet or soy ice cream): 164
Total Fat as % of Daily Value: 7%
Protein: 2 gm   Fat: 5 gm   Carbohydrates: 30 gm   Calcium: 21 mg
Iron: 1 mg   Sodium: 155 mg   Dietary Fiber: 2 gm

Crock Pot Cherry Cobbler
(Makes 4 servings)

Pull this dish together the night before, so you can turn on the crock pot the minute you walk in the door after work or school.

1 can (about 16 ounces) cherry pie filling
1 cup vegan yellow cake mix
1/8 cup softened vegan margarine
1/4 cup chopped nuts
Sorbet or soy ice cream, as desired

Pour cherry pie filling into a crock pot, spreading it evenly across the bottom of the crock. In a medium-sized bowl, combine cake mix and margarine until the mixture is crumbly. Sprinkle evenly over cherries. Sprinkle nuts evenly over cake mix.

Set crock pot on low, cover, and allow it to cook for 3 hours. Serve hot, right from the crock pot, or serve it over sorbet, if desired.

Note: Any fruit pie filling will do. Refrigerate extra portions of this cobbler and mix it into hot oatmeal, yogurt, or tofu for a breakfast treat.

Total Calories Per Serving Using Walnuts (minus frozen dessert): 466
Total Fat as % of Daily Value: 25%
Protein: 4 gm   Fat: 16 gm   Carbohydrates: 80 gm   Calcium: 35 mg
Iron: 2 mg   Sodium: 436 mg   Dietary Fiber: 2 gm

Almond Rice Pudding

(Makes 3 servings)

Here's a great way to include rice and fruit in your meal.

1/2 cup uncooked white or brown rice
1 cup water
2 cups almond milk (you can substitute plain or vanilla
**   soy or rice milk with 1 Tablespoon almond extract)**
1/4 cup maple syrup
1/2 teaspoon vanilla extract
1 teaspoon cinnamon
1/4 cup raisins, dried cranberries, or dried blueberries

In a medium-sized saucepan, combine rice and water. Bring to a fast boil, cover, and reduce heat. Simmer for 15 minutes or until all the water is absorbed. Stir in almond milk and maple syrup, stirring, until the rice mixture is as thick as soupy cooked cereal (this should take approximately 30 minutes). Remove from heat and stir in cinnamon and raisins or other dried fruit. Eat warm or refrigerate until you're ready to eat.

Note: Pudding, if overcooked, will become dry instead of creamy.

Total Calories Per Serving Using Brown Rice: 301
Total Fat as % of Daily Value: 6%
Protein: 8 gm   Fat: 4 gm   Carbohydrates: 55 gm   Calcium: 50 mg
Iron: 2 mg   Sodium: 25 mg   Dietary Fiber: 4 gm

Frozen Berry Banana "Ice Cream"
(Makes 2 servings)

What a terrific way to use extra bananas!

2 ripe bananas
1 cup fresh or thawed, frozen berries
1 Tablespoon apple juice concentrate or maple syrup
1/4 teaspoon cinnamon
1/4 teaspoon ginger

In a medium-sized bowl, mash fruit together. Transfer fruit and remaining ingredients in a blender and process until just smooth. Pour into individual serving dishes, plastic containers, or ice cube trays, and freeze for 1 hour before eating.

Total Calories Per Serving Using Blueberries and Concentrate: 164
Total Fat as % of Daily Value: 2%
Protein: 2 gm   Fat: 1 gm   Carbohydrates: 41 gm   Calcium: 19 mg
Iron: 1 mg   Sodium: 4 mg   Dietary Fiber: 5 gm

Frozen Tropicale

(Makes 1 serving)

This tastes too good to be so good for you.

1/2 cup soy fruit-flavored yogurt
1/4 cup orange juice
1/2 cup canned pineapple tidbits, drained
**1/8 cup mandarin oranges or fresh mango cubes, if
    desired**

Combine yogurt, orange juice, pineapple, and oranges or mango
(if desired) in a blender and blend until smooth. Pour into individual serving dishes, plastic containers, or ice cube trays, and
freeze for 1 hour before eating.

Total Calories Per Serving Using Mandarin Oranges: 193
Total Fat as % of Daily Value: 9%
Protein: 8 gm   Fat: 6 gm   Carbohydrates: 28 gm   Calcium: 168 mg
Iron: 8 mg   Sodium: 20 mg   Dietary Fiber: 3 gm

SNACKS

Your Own Personal Power Bar
(Makes approximately 10 large or 20 small bars)

Forget the commercial bars – you can make your own!

1 cup crumbled shredded wheat-type cereal
1 teaspoon fresh orange zest
1/4 cup raisins
1/4 cup chopped walnuts, pecans, or hulled sunflower seeds
1/2 cup cornflake or bran flake cereal
1/2 cup chopped dates or figs
1/4 cup vegan dry sweetener
1/4 cup mashed firm tofu
1/2 cup chopped pitted prunes
1/3 cup vegan graham cracker crumbs

In a medium-sized mixing bowl, combine shredded wheat, orange zest, raisins, nuts, flakes, and figs. Mix until combined. Set aside.

In a medium-sized saucepan, combine sweetener, tofu, and prunes. Stir over medium heat for approximately 5 minutes, or until the mixture thickens (don't burn it!). Combine cereal mixture with heated mixture. Allow mixture to cool sufficiently before forming it into individual logs or bars on a clean work surface. Measure 2 Tablespoons for a small bar, 4 Tablespoons for a large bar. Roll each bar in graham cracker crumbs. Place bars in a tightly-covered plastic storage container. Refrigerate for at least 2 hours before eating. Bars will last 5 days in a refrigerator.

Total Calories Per Large Bar Using Walnuts and Bran Flakes: 144
Total Fat as % of Daily Value: 5%
Protein: 3 gm   Fat: 3 gm   Carbohydrates: 29 gm   Calcium: 36 mg
Iron: 2 mg   Sodium: 45 mg   Dietary Fiber: 3 gm

Carrot Orange Cookies

(Make 30 small cookies)

These cookies can be part of breakfast or lunch, paired with some fruit or vegetable sticks.

1-1/3 cups carrots, chopped
3/4 cup vegan margarine
3/4 cup vegan granulated sweetener
2 teaspoons soft tofu
1 Tablespoon orange juice
1 teaspoon vanilla
1 teaspoon fresh or dried orange zest
2 cups all purpose flour
1 teaspoon baking powder
2/3 cup chopped walnuts or Brazil nuts
Vegetable oil spray

Preheat oven to 350 degrees. Place carrots in a small pot or in the microwave and cook until very soft. Purée in a blender or food processor.

In a large bowl, combine margarine with sweetener. Add tofu and juice and mix well. Stir in vanilla and zest. In a separate bowl, mix flour and baking powder. Alternately, add the margarine mixture, puréed carrots, and flour mixture until totally mixed.

Spray baking sheets with vegetable oil. Drop cookie batter by Tablespoonfuls onto sheets. Bake at 350 degrees approximately 15 minutes, or until springy to the touch. Can be stored in the refrigerator until ready to use.

Total Calories Per Cookie Using Walnuts: 111
Total Fat as % of Daily Value: 10%
Protein: 1 gm   Fat: 6 gm   Carbohydrates: 13 gm   Calcium: 16 mg
Iron: 1 mg   Sodium: 72 mg   Dietary Fiber: 1 gm

Peanut Butter-Graham Roundies

(Makes approximately 15 roundies)

You probably already have all the ingredients for this recipe either in your pantry or refrigerator.

1-1/2 cups vegan graham cracker crumbs
2/3 cup smooth peanut butter
1 teaspoon vanilla
1/4 cup vanilla soy or rice milk (plain is okay, too)
2 teaspoons vegan dry sweetener
1/2 cup crushed dry cereal (we like Rice Krispies or
    flakes)

If the graham cracker crumbs are large, crush them into very small pieces. In a medium bowl, mix peanut butter, vanilla, milk, and sweetener until smooth. Add crumbs slowly and mix until thoroughly combined.

    Spread cereal on a plate or other clean surface. Form peanut butter mixture into small, round balls and roll in dry cereal until coated. Refrigerate for at least 1 hour before eating.

Note: Try this with hazelnut, almond, or soy butter instead of peanut butter.

Total Calories Per Roundie Using Soymilk: 127
Total Fat as % of Daily Value: 11%
Protein: 4 gm   Fat: 7 gm   Carbohydrates: 13 gm   Calcium: 11 mg
Iron: 1 mg   Sodium: 134 mg   Dietary Fiber: 1 gm

Striped Parfait

(Makes 3 servings)

Leftovers never tasted so good.

1 small box (3.5-ounce) instant vegan pudding mix
1-1/2 cups soy, rice, or nut milk
1/2 teaspoon vanilla extract
1 cup fresh or thawed, frozen strawberries, sliced
1 cup leftover vegan cake, cut into cubes
1/3 cup shredded coconut
1/3 cup fresh or thawed, frozen blueberries (optional)

Prepare pudding according to package directions, using milk and extract. Allow pudding to chill for 30 minutes.

To assemble parfaits, layer pudding, strawberries, cake, and coconut, ending with pudding. Top with blueberries, if desired. Refrigerate until ready to use.

Note: You can use softened sorbet instead of pudding; if not intended for immediate consumption, parfaits can be frozen for later use.

Total Calories Per Serving Using Soymilk and Optional Blueberries: 271
Total Fat as % of Daily Value: 11%
Protein: 5 gm   Fat: 7 gm   Carbohydrates: 50 gm   Calcium: 23 mg
Iron: 1 mg   Sodium: 575 mg   Dietary Fiber: 4 gm

Pineapple and Baked Beans Dip

(Makes approximately 1 cup or 8 servings)

Use as a dip for crackers or as a filling for a sandwich.

6 ounces firm tofu
1/4 cup canned crushed pineapple, drained
1/2 cup canned vegetarian baked beans
2 Tablespoons chopped green onions or 2 teaspoons onion powder
1 Tablespoon red pepper flakes
Crackers, chips, or veggies for dipping

Place tofu in a medium-sized mixing bowl and mash. Add remaining ingredients and mix until thoroughly combined. Allow mixture to chill in the refrigerator for at least 1 hour before serving.

Total Calories Per 2 Tablespoons Dip: 55
Total Fat as % of Daily Value: 3%
Protein: 4 gm   Fat: 2 gm   Carbohydrates: 6 gm   Calcium: 55 mg
Iron: 2 mg   Sodium: 67 mg   Dietary Fiber: 2 gm

Baked Veggie Chips
(Makes approximately 6 servings)

Enjoy this rainbow of chips.

**3 pounds washed, unpeeled red rose or white rose
   boiling potatoes, carrots, beets, or taro, sliced
   into 1/4-inch thick slices**
Vegetable oil spray
Dried herbs of choice (see note below)

Preheat oven to 475 degrees. Place veggies, in a single layer, on nonstick baking sheets (if nonstick sheets are not available, spray sheets with vegetable oil). Generously spray veggies with oil.

   Bake at 475 degrees for 5 minutes, rotating sheets if baking is not even. Remove from oven (only briefly), sprinkle with herbs, return to oven, and continue to bake until crisp and brown, about 7 minutes. Transfer to a plate or platter and eat hot or allow to cool (they will not stay crisp, but are still tasty).

Note: Some people just sprinkle these with salt and pepper, some like chili powder or red pepper flakes, some go the garlic powder route, and some use herb blends.

Total Calories Per Serving Using 1 Pound Potatoes, Carrots, and Beets: 131
Total Fat as % of Daily Value: 2%
Protein: 4 gm   Fat: 1 gm   Carbohydrates: 28gm   Calcium: 38 mg
Iron: 2 mg   Sodium: 90 mg   Dietary Fiber: 6 gm

Mediterranean Artichoke Nibblers
(Makes approximately 12 pieces or 6 servings)

Prepare these to pamper yourself.

1 can (13-14 ounces) artichoke hearts, drained and chopped
1/3 cup Italian salad dressing
3 ounces silken tofu
2 Tablespoons chopped pimentos or chopped red bell peppers
1 Tablespoon chopped fresh parsley
12 vegan crackers (your choice)

Place artichokes, salad dressing, and tofu in a medium-sized bowl and beat with an electric mixer until very well blended. Stir in pimentos and parsley. Chill for at least 1 hour in the refrigerator. When ready to eat, spread on crackers.

Total Calories Per Serving Using Pimentos (minus crackers): 98
Total Fat as % of Daily Value: 10%
Protein: 2 gm   Fat: 7 gm   Carbohydrates: 7 gm   Calcium: 8 mg
Iron: 1 mg   Sodium: 310 mg   Dietary Fiber: 1 gm

Crackers and Herbs

(Makes spread for approximately 10 crackers or 5 servings)

Here's a low fat, flavorful snack.

1/8 cup olive oil
2 teaspoons tomato paste
1/2 teaspoon chopped fresh parsley
1/4 teaspoon dried basil
1/4 teaspoon dried oregano
1/4 teaspoon granulated garlic
1/4 teaspoon dried rosemary
10 vegan crackers, saltine-sized

In a medium-sized, nonreactive bowl, combine all ingredients except crackers. Mix well, refrigerate, and allow spread to chill for at least 2 hours before eating. Serve on crackers or on sliced veggies.

Note: This snack gets better after a day in the refrigerator, and will last for up to 4 days in the refrigerator.

Total Calories Per Serving (minus crackers): 51
Total Fat as % of Daily Value: 8%
Protein: <1 gm   Fat: 5 gm   Carbohydrates: 1 gm   Calcium: 5 mg
Iron: <1 mg   Sodium: 2 mg   Dietary Fiber: <1 gm

Chili Snack Crunch
(Makes 5 cups or 5 servings)

Enjoy the great texture and spicy flavor!

3 cups popped popcorn
1 cup snack crackers, crumbled into big pieces (see note)
1/4 cup hulled sunflower seeds
1/2 cup raisins
1 Tablespoon oil or melted vegan margarine
2 teaspoons chili powder
1/2 teaspoon red pepper flakes

In a medium-sized bowl, mix popcorn, crackers, seeds, and raisins. In a small bowl or cup, mix oil, chili powder, and flakes. Toss popcorn and spices together until well coated. Store in an airtight container in a cool place (but not the refrigerator, as the oil will harden).

Note: This is a great place to use leftover crackers. You can use plain crackers (like saltines), pretzels, or spicy crackers (we've seen cracked pepper crackers and salsa-flavored crackers).

Total Calories Per Serving: 183   Total Fat as % of Daily Value: 14%
Protein: 4 gm   Fat: 9 gm   Carbohydrates: 24 gm   Calcium: 32 mg
Iron: 2 mg   Sodium: 110 mg   Dietary Fiber: 2 gm

Brochettes

(Makes 3 skewers)

Use as appetizers or a fast snack.

5 ounces fresh or thawed, frozen vegan tortellini, ravioli, or gnocchi
1/4 cup vegan soy sour cream (see glossary)
1/4 cup tomato or pizza sauce
1/2 teaspoon granulated garlic
1/2 teaspoon dried basil
6 cherry tomatoes
Vegetable oil spray

Cook tortellini, ravioli, or gnocchi according to directions on package. Drain and set aside.

In a small pot, combine remaining ingredients and cook until heated through; keep warm.

On bamboo or metal skewers, arrange tortellini, ravioli, or gnocchi and tomatoes. Spray a medium-sized frying pan with oil and allow to heat. Place skewers in the pan and allow to cook, turning, until tomatoes are beginning to get soft and the tortellini, ravioli, or gnocchi are hot. Serve sauce as a dip.

Total Calories Per Serving Using Vegan Potato Gnocchi: 110
Total Fat as % of Daily Value: 2%
Protein: 3 gm   Fat: 1 gm   Carbohydrates: 22 gm   Calcium: 17 mg
Iron: 1 mg   Sodium: 308 mg   Dietary Fiber: 1 gm

Chapter Eight

Every Day and Special Day Cooking

You deserve good food every day – why save the best stuff only for guests? In this chapter, we've included easy recipes that require only a few ingredients. They'll be simple to toss together after a long day. We've also included recipes that may require a bit more time and feature not-every-day ingredients for those days when you feel like indulging yourself, or when you're cooking for company. None of the recipes takes more than 20 or 30 minutes to prepare (cooking or cooling time may be longer). Most take only 10 to 15 minutes.

Although most of the recipes in this volume are written for 2 hearty servings, they can easily be doubled for larger parties or intentional leftovers.

Complementing these recipes for a full, pleasant meal is simple to do. Cook a white or sweet potato in the oven or the microwave, steam some fresh or frozen veggies in the steamer or in the microwave, or just slice some fresh raw fruit or veggies to have with these dishes. Freshly sliced bell peppers, carrots, jicama, avocado, pears, apples, oranges, grapefruit, pineapple, grapes, and berries are flavorful accompaniments for hot dishes. If you're feeling creative, choose from apples, pears, pineapples, onions, peppers, or summer squash (zucchini or yellow squash), slice and toss the pieces into a frying pan with margarine and black pepper. Sauté until slices have reached the degree of tenderness you prefer. If you like to cook with wine, port, or sherry, splash a bit on this dish just before it's finished and let the added liquid cook until it has evaporated.

Remember your spice rack, and if you're really ambitious, your herb garden. If all you want is a bowl of cauliflower or broccoli for dinner, spice it up, at least, with vinegar, garlic, and pepper. Shake an herb-blend into some rice and toss in some thawed or canned veggies for a fast pseudo-pilaf. Have salsa, chutney, nutritional yeast, chopped nuts, seeds (like sesame and sunflower), and vegan croutons on hand to build up a salad, soup, or bowl of grains.

If you don't even feel like following a recipe, learn how to create your own dishes from what you store in the refrigerator and the pantry. Combine two different types of canned beans with salsa and hot sauce for a fast microwave chili; serve it over a baked potato or some rice. Combine several types of frozen veggies with margarine and steam or sauté them with your favorite herbs. Add canned lentils or cubes of tofu, cover with vegan cheese, and bake. Place cubes of tofu or seitan in a baking dish, cover with barbecue sauce, and bake until hot. Pair them with a fruit or veggie salad, and you've made dinner.

You'll find more on barbecuing in a special section of this chapter. The key to barbecuing is to take advantage of those coals! Plan ahead and barbecue meals to eat for several days. A hibachi is a good way to prepare several hot meals without heating up the kitchen during hot months. Purchase seasonal produce and buy a bit more than you'll use in one day. Barbecued veggies hold well in the refrigerator for several days and taste good hot or cold. Grilled veggies can be chopped and added to soups, cold salads, and sandwiches. Grill some firm tofu, mix with vegan mayonnaise, chopped celery and onions, olives, and relish and you've got a cold salad you can use for sandwich fillings or to top entrée salads.

Select recipes that suit each other. Perhaps you favor corn, but you probably wouldn't want to choose three recipes containing corn to be served at one meal. Pace yourself. Plan to use ingredients you have in the house. Contain your excitement and creativity and use up what's leftover before buying a whole new round of ingredients. You should be able to see around your freezer, it shouldn't be a search-and-seek expedition.

Kebobs or brochettes can be cooked on the barbecue, in a hot oven, or under a broiler. Invest in some bamboo or metal skewers (we've been known to use wooden chopsticks in a pinch!). Use rosemary branches as skewers, If you can find them (or know someone who grows them). They're aromatic and strong enough to hold up to heat. Skewer combos of cherry tomatoes, button mushrooms, slices of bell peppers or carrots, wedges of onion, cubes of tofu, seitan, or tempeh, or cubes of pineapple, daikon radish, steamed potatoes, or taro. Marinate in Italian dressing, lemon and chopped herbs, wine and herbs, or commercially prepared marinades. Throw them on the grill, in a very hot oven (425 degrees is good), or under a hot broiler, and let them cook away while you kick back and watch. While the barbecue grill is hot, we like to wrap a couple of peeled onions in foil (you can add vegan margarine, pepper, or wine) and let them steam right on the grill. Use these onions throughout the week instead of raw or sautéed onions. If you're brave (or just into fire), roast potatoes right in the coals for a smoky flavor. A final tip: roast fresh bell peppers or chilies on the grill until their skins are blackened. Peel away the skin and you've got intense pepper flavor you can use in dishes throughout the week.

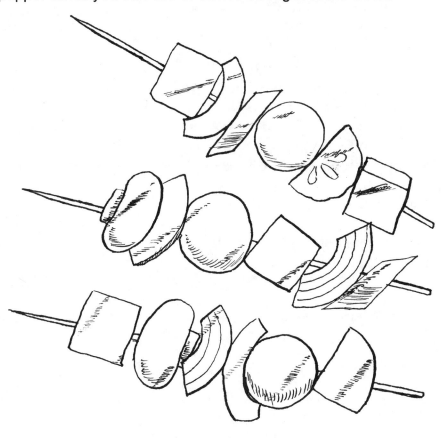

Entrées

Multi-Colored Pasta with Broccoli
(Makes 2 servings)

This dish is colorful, crunchy, and can be eaten hot or cold.

Vegetable oil spray
1 cup fresh or thawed, frozen broccoli florets
1/4 cup diced bell pepper (any color is fine)
2 diced green onions
1 minced garlic clove
1 teaspoon garlic powder
**1/2 cup thawed, frozen chopped spinach, drained, or
    3/4 cup fresh spinach, chopped**
**1 cup cooked tricolored pasta, such as fusilli or twists
    (or 1/3 cup uncooked pasta)**
1/2 cup cherry tomatoes, halved
1/8 cup sliced black olives
1 Tablespoon vinegar
1 teaspoon dried basil

Heat a large pot over medium heat and spray with oil. Add broccoli, pepper, onions, and garlic and sauté until the broccoli is tender, approximately 5 minutes. Add spinach and allow it to wilt, approximately 1 minute. Remove pot from heat and add pasta, olives, vinegar, and basil. Toss to combine. Eat immediately, or chill until ready to serve as a cold dish.

Total Calories Per Serving: 90   Total Fat as % of Daily Value: 3%
Protein: 4 gm   Fat: 2 gm   Carbohydrates: 16 gm   Calcium: 81 mg
Iron: 2 mg   Sodium: 111 mg   Dietary Fiber: 3 gm

Italian Tofu with Mushrooms and Peppers
(Makes 2 servings)

This dish is aromatic and can be eaten on its own or paired with pasta. As a leftover it can be stuffed in a pita or put on top of a salad.

1 teaspoon olive oil or vegetable oil spray
1 small bell pepper, chopped (about 1/4 cup)
1/4 cup chopped onions
1 minced garlic clove or 1 teaspoon garlic powder
6 ounces firm tofu, drained and cubed
1 cup mushrooms, drained and sliced
1 Tablespoon vinegar (balsamic tastes best in this recipe)
1/2 teaspoon dried oregano
1/2 teaspoon red pepper flakes

In a medium-sized frying pan, heat oil over medium heat. Add peppers, onions, and garlic and sauté for 5 minutes or until soft. Add tofu and mushrooms, tossing and stirring. Reduce heat to a simmer. Add vinegar, oregano, and red pepper and simmer for 2 minutes. Voila, dinner!

Note: This recipe can be eaten hot or cold and served over mashed or baked potatoes, rice, or pasta. You can purchase frozen chopped bell peppers; so that you can measure out only what you need and freeze the rest with no waste. Of course, if you have leftover fresh bell pepper, you can throw it in a salad, in soups, in sandwiches, on cooked veggies, in tofu scrambles, and on top of pizza. The same goes for any extra onions, garlic, or mushrooms.

Total Calories Per Serving: 181   Total Fat as % of Daily Value: 15%
Protein: 15 gm   Fat: 10 gm   Carbohydrates: 12 gm   Calcium: 158 mg
Iron: 10 mg   Sodium: 18 mg   Dietary Fiber: 4 gm

Pasta with Sun-Dried Tomatoes and Wild Mushrooms
(Makes 2 servings)

Indulge yourself or surprise your guests with this recipe. It's simple to make; the secret is the tomatoes and mushrooms.

1 Tablespoon vegan margarine
1 Tablespoon chopped onions
1/2 cup fresh wild mushrooms (see note below), cut into quarters or small pieces
6 whole sun-dried tomatoes, sliced into thin strips
1 cup vegan sour cream (see glossary)
1/2 cup water
1 teaspoon white pepper
1/2 pound fresh (not dried) pasta, such as angel hair or fettuccini
1 green onion, cut lengthwise into strips

Melt margarine in a large frying pan over medium heat. Add onions; continue to cook and stir for 1 minute. Add mushrooms and tomatoes; continue to cook and stir for 3 minutes. Add sour cream and water. Season with pepper. Bring to a fast boil, reduce heat, and simmer until sauce is thick enough to coat a spoon, approximately 4 minutes.

Bring a pot of water to a boil and cook fresh pasta until just tender (*al dente*), approximately 3 minutes. Drain. In a large bowl, toss pasta with sauce and garnish with onions.

Note: Most market's produce sections offer wild mushrooms. Try porcini, shiitake, oyster, chanterelle, or lobster mushrooms for different flavors, colors, and textures. Fresh button or portobello mushrooms will do as well. If you have dried wild mushrooms in your pantry, you can reconstitute them (be sure they are soft) and use the leftover water for what's needed in this recipe. Purchase sun-dried tomatoes in vacuum-packed bags; they have a better taste than those packed in brine or oil. If you have no fresh pasta on hand, you can use dried pasta. Be sure to cook dried pasta longer than fresh pasta.

Total Calories Per Serving: 465   Total Fat as % of Daily Value: 21%
Protein: 18 gm   Fat: 14 gm   Carbohydrates: 70 gm   Calcium: 165 mg
Iron: 11 mg   Sodium: 379 mg   Dietary Fiber: 6 gm

Confetti Pasta
(Makes 2 servings)

You can judge this recipe by its cover – it's colorful and flavorful.

Vegetable oil spray
1 cup frozen, thawed or steamed fresh asparagus spears, chopped
1/2 cup chopped yellow squash
1/4 cup chopped red bell pepper
1 cup cooked pasta (small shapes, such as small shells, bow ties, and penne)
1 Tablespoon vegan margarine
2 Tablespoons shredded vegan soy cheese or sour cream (see glossary)
1 Tablespoon chopped green olives
1/2 teaspoon nutmeg
1/2 teaspoon white pepper

Heat a medium-sized frying pan and spray with oil. Add asparagus, squash, and pepper and sauté for 1 minute. Add pasta, margarine, vegan cheese, olives, nutmeg, and pepper and cook, stirring and tossing, until heated and cheese is melted.

Total Calories Per Serving: 181   Total Fat as % of Daily Value: 13%
Protein: 5 gm   Fat: 8 gm   Carbohydrates: 23 gm   Calcium: 52 mg
Iron: 2 mg   Sodium: 257 mg   Dietary Fiber: 3 gm

Almost Thai Spicy Peanut Pasta

(Makes 2 servings)

Make this dish as hot or mild as you like for a change of pace pasta.

4 ounces uncooked fettuccini or angel hair pasta
1/2 cup peeled carrots, cut into thin strips
1/2 cup frozen peas, thawed
2 Tablespoons vinegar
2 teaspoons red pepper flakes
1 teaspoon hot sauce
2 Tablespoons oil
1 teaspoon soy sauce
1 Tablespoon orange juice concentrate
1-1/2 Tablespoons smooth peanut butter

Cook fettuccini according to package directions. Drain and set aside.

Steam or microwave carrots and peas until tender. Drain and set aside.

In a small pot or in a microwave dish, combine vinegar, red pepper flakes, hot sauce, oil, soy sauce, orange juice concentrate, and peanut butter. Cook over medium heat and stir until smooth, or microwave on high for 1 minute. After cooking, whisk for a very smooth sauce.

In a medium-sized bowl, combine pasta, carrots, peas, and sauce. Toss to coat pasta. Serve hot or cold.

Total Calories Per Serving: 473   Total Fat as % of Daily Value: 33%
Protein: 19 gm   Fat: 22 gm   Carbohydrates: 53 gm   Calcium: 51 mg
Iron: 4 mg   Sodium: 297 mg   Dietary Fiber: 6 gm

Red Pepper and Pine Nut Orzo
(Makes 2 servings)

This dish is both a comfort food and an elegant meal.

Vegetable oil spray
2 Tablespoons pine nuts
1/8 cup chopped fresh red pepper
1 chopped green onion
1 cup cooked orzo (about 1/3 cup uncooked)
1 teaspoon red pepper flakes

Spray a medium-sized frying pan with oil and allow to heat. Add pine nuts and toast until light brown and fragrant, approximately 5 minutes. Remove from pan.

Add red pepper and green onion to pan and cook until soft, approximately 2 minutes. Mix in orzo and red pepper flakes; cook and stir until heated through.

Note: You should be able to find orzo or pastina in most grocery stores. Orzo is pasta that is shaped like a fat grain of rice; its cousin, pastina, is shaped like tiny stars, and can also be used. Uncooked, both look more like cereal or grain, rather than pasta. Cooked with margarine, sweetener, and cinnamon, orzo and pastina make a tasty hot breakfast. Both can be used instead of rice in rice pudding, too.

Total Calories Per Serving: 198   Total Fat as % of Daily Value: 9%
Protein: 7 gm   Fat: 6 gm   Carbohydrates: 30 gm   Calcium: 11 mg
Iron: 2 mg   Sodium: 6 mg   Dietary Fiber: 3 gm

Potato Tacos
(Makes 3 tacos)

Have fun! The potatoes you prepared at breakfast can be used for a flavorful lunch or dinner.

Vegetable oil spray
1/2 cup frozen or fresh raw hash brown potatoes
1/2 teaspoon cumin
1/2 teaspoon chili powder
1/2 teaspoon black pepper
1/4 cup shredded vegan soy cheese
1 chopped green onion
1/2 cup tempeh, seitan, or fake meat strips (cut tempeh or seitan into thin strips)
2 Tablespoons canned cut corn or thawed, frozen cut corn, drained
2 shredded Romaine leaves
3 taco shells or tortillas
Salsa, as desired

Spray a medium-sized frying pan with oil and heat. Cook hash browns until very crispy. Season with cumin, chili, and pepper. Remove from heat, place in a medium-sized bowl, and toss with vegan cheese and onions. Cook tempeh in same pan, adding onions and cooking until onions are soft and tempeh is heated. Assemble tacos with potatoes, tempeh, and lettuce on taco shells or wrapped into tortillas. Top with salsa, if desired.

Total Calories Per Serving Using Tempeh (minus salsa): 368
Total Fat as % of Daily Value: 17%
Protein: 13 gm   Fat: 11 gm   Carbohydrates: 55 gm   Calcium: 151 mg
Iron: 4 mg   Sodium: 362 mg   Dietary Fiber: 5 gm

Red Potato, Mustard Green, and Mushroom Sauté

(Makes 2 servings)

Eat your greens! This recipe makes it easy.

2 medium red potatoes (any type of small boiling potato will do)
Vegetable oil spray
1/2 cup sliced fresh mushrooms
1 teaspoon black pepper
2 cups (packed) mustard greens or kale

Steam or microwave potatoes until soft (here's another good place to use your leftover cooked potatoes). Heat a large frying pan and spray with oil. Quarter potatoes and add with mushrooms to pan. Season with pepper. Cook and stir until potatoes are hot and mushrooms are soft, approximately 5 minutes. Add greens and cook and stir until wilted, approximately 2 minutes. Serve immediately.

Total Calories Per Serving Using Mustard Greens: 88
Total Fat as % of Daily Value: 1%
Protein: 4 gm   Fat: 1 gm   Carbohydrates: 18 gm   Calcium: 69 mg
Iron: 2 mg   Sodium: 20 mg   Dietary Fiber: 4 gm

Tofu (or Seitan or Tempeh) Aztec
(Makes 2 servings)

You don't have to hike Mexican ruins to discover the secrets of Aztec cuisine. This dish is an interesting combination of sweet prunes and salty olives.

Vegetable oil spray
1/4 cup chopped onions
1 medium baking potato, peeled and cubed
1 carrot, peeled and sliced
1/2 cup vegetable broth or water
1/3 cup chopped pitted prunes
1/3 cup sliced green olives
1/4 cup orange juice concentrate
1 bay leaf
1 cup cubed tofu, seitan, or tempeh ("chicken-flavored" or smoked is fine)

Heat a large pot and spray with oil. Add onions and cook until brown, approximately 5 minutes. Add remaining ingredients, except tofu, seitan, or tempeh. Cover and allow to simmer for 30 minutes or until potatoes and carrots are soft. Remove bay leaf and add tofu, seitan, or tempeh. Cover again and allow dish to cook for 10 minutes longer. Serve warm.

Total Calories Per Serving Using Tofu: 437
Total Fat as % of Daily Value: 23%
Protein: 24 gm   Fat: 15 gm   Carbohydrates: 60 gm   Calcium: 263 mg
Iron: 15 mg   Sodium: 797 mg   Dietary Fiber: 8 gm

Peanut-Tofu Stew
(Makes 2 servings)

This recipe has African influences. Beware that it is high fat!

Vegetable oil spray
1/4 cup chopped onions
1/4 cup chopped celery
1/8 cup flour
2 cups vegetable broth
1/2 cup creamy peanut butter (do not use chunky style)
1 cup plain vegan soy yogurt or sour cream (see glossary)
1 cup cubed firm tofu
2 teaspoons granulated garlic

Heat a large pot and spray with oil. Add onions and celery and sauté over medium heat until brown, approximately 5 minutes. Add flour and stir to combine. Add broth, bring to a boil, and reduce heat. Allow mixture to simmer until thickened, approximately 25 minutes. Whisk in peanut butter and yogurt or sour cream. Continue to whisk and stir, or put soup in a blender and purée until smooth, then return to pot. Add tofu and garlic and allow stew to cook for 10 minutes. Serve warm.

Total Calories Per Serving Using Soy Yogurt: 729
Total Fat as % of Daily Value: 78%
Protein: 46 gm   Fat: 51 gm   Carbohydrates: 36 gm   Calcium: 381 mg
Iron: 22 mg   Sodium: 1340 mg   Dietary Fiber: 9 gm

Mediterranean Stuffed Veggies

(Makes 2 servings)

Visit the South of France with this recipe.

2 medium bell peppers, yellow squash, or onions
1/2 cup frozen chopped spinach, thawed, or cooked, cooled fresh spinach
1/8 cup chopped green olives
1/2 cup vegan croutons or 1 slice fresh bread, cut into cubes
2 teaspoons dried basil or 1 teaspoon fresh chopped basil
3 Tablespoons vegan soy sour cream (see glossary)
1 teaspoon black pepper
1 small onion, cut into rings

Preheat oven to 425 degrees. Place whole veggies on a rack and roast for 20 minutes or until skins begin to blister, but not blacken. Remove from oven, cut off tops of peppers, and deseed (or peel onions and scoop out center or cut squash in half lengthwise and scoop out center).

In a large bowl, combine remaining ingredients, except onion rings. Fill each veggie, packing the filling in tightly. Place veggies in a baking dish. Top with onion rings. Cover and heat at 425 degrees for 20 minutes or until heated through.

Note: You can substitute 10 large button mushrooms or 1 large portobello mushroom or 2 medium zucchini for the bell peppers, yellow squash, or onions.

Total Calories Per Serving Using Bell Peppers: 112
Total Fat as % of Daily Value: 4%
Protein: 5 gm   Fat: 3 gm   Carbohydrates: 19 gm   Calcium: 117 mg
Iron: 3 mg   Sodium: 302 mg   Dietary Fiber: 5 gm

Asian Sautéed Eggplant
(Makes 2 servings)

This fast recipe has flavor and texture that won't stop!

**1 Tablespoon oil (for authentic Asian taste, use peanut
   or sesame oil)**
1/2 Tablespoon diced onions
2 cups peeled and cubed eggplant
1 Tablespoon soy sauce
1 teaspoon red pepper flakes
1 teaspoon minced fresh garlic
**1 Tablespoon vinegar (for authentic Asian taste, use
   rice vinegar)**
1/4 cup vegetable broth
1 teaspoon sesame seeds (if desired)

Heat oil in a large frying pan over medium-high heat. Add onions
and cook until soft, approximately 2 minutes. Add eggplant and
toss over medium-high heat so cubes are coated and oil is
absorbed, approximately 2 minutes. Add soy sauce, red pepper,
garlic, vinegar, and broth and reduce to simmer. Cover and allow
to cook until eggplant is tender, approximately 8 minutes. Stir in
sesame seeds, if desired, and enjoy!

Total Calories Per Serving: 107   Total Fat as % of Daily Value: 12%
Protein: 3 gm   Fat: 8 gm   Carbohydrates: 8 gm   Calcium: 27 mg
Iron: 1 mg   Sodium: 632 mg   Dietary Fiber: 3 gm

Drunken Carrots with Tofu

(Makes 2 servings)

Don't wait for St. Patrick's Day for this one; you may want to save a little beer for the cook.

1 Tablespoon vegan margarine
1 cup peeled carrots, sliced on the diagonal
3/4 cup beer (Guinness stout or Bass Ale works well)
1/2 cup cubed firm plain or smoked tofu
1 teaspoon dried dill
1/2 teaspoon vegan dried sweetener
1/2 teaspoon salt

Heat a medium-sized frying pan over medium heat and melt margarine. Add carrots and sauté until glazed, approximately 2 minutes. Add beer, reduce heat, cover, and cook until carrots are tender (stirring frequently), approximately 12 minutes. Stir in tofu and dill and cook for 1 more minute. Sprinkle with sweetener and salt, turn heat up to high and cook, uncovered, until almost all the liquid is evaporated, approximately 3 minutes. Eat immediately.

Note: This dish does not cool well, so plan your eating time with its cooking time.

Total Calories Per Serving: 213   Total Fat as % of Daily Value: 17%
Protein: 11 gm   Fat: 11 gm   Carbohydrates: 14 gm   Calcium: 458 mg
Iron: 7 mg   Sodium: 681 mg   Dietary Fiber: 3 gm

Quick Tofu Stroganoff
(Makes 2 servings)

Catherine the Great would be proud – Some Russian cuisine for the new century.

Vegetable oil spray
1 cup sliced fresh mushrooms
1/2 cup thinly sliced onions
1 Tablespoon flour
1 cup vegetable broth
1 cup cubed firm tofu, seitan, or tempeh
3/4 cup vegan soy sour cream (see glossary)
1 teaspoon pepper

Spray a large pot with oil and heat. Add mushrooms and onions and sauté until onions are translucent, approximately 4 minutes. Stir in flour to coat veggies. Slowly stir in broth and simmer until thickened, approximately 10 minutes. Mix in tofu and cook until thoroughly heated, approximately 5 minutes. Add sour cream, stir and heat for 5 minutes (do not allow dish to boil). Serve warm.

Total Calories Per Serving Using Tofu: 311
Total Fat as % of Daily Value: 25%
Protein: 28 gm   Fat: 17 gm   Carbohydrates: 20 gm   Calcium: 978 mg
Iron: 20 mg   Sodium: 528 mg   Dietary Fiber: 5 gm

Upscale Greens with Avocado and Chilies

(Makes 2 servings)

This salad has some bite to it, with the combination of bitter greens and chilies; pair it with a mild entrée and a sweet dessert. Beware that this dish is high fat!

1 Tablespoon lemon juice
2 teaspoons granulated garlic or 1/2 minced garlic clove
1/8 cup olive oil
2 Tablespoons chopped fresh cilantro or parsley
1 ripe avocado, peeled, halved, and pitted
1 small head escarole, curly endive, or green endive, torn into bite-size pieces
1/8 cup chopped red pepper or fresh red chili

In a small bowl, combine lemon juice and garlic. Whisk in oil and add cilantro or parsley.

Cut avocados into thin slices and arrange on a plate. Spoon dressing over the avocado and let sit in the refrigerator for at least 30 minutes (you can do this the night before, if you like). Place lettuce in a medium bowl. Arrange avocado on top and spoon remaining dressing (from avocado plate) on top. Garnish with peppers. Chill until ready to eat.

Total Calories Per Serving Using Parsley: 332
Total Fat as % of Daily Value: 45%
Protein: 5 gm   Fat: 29 gm   Carbohydrates: 18 gm   Calcium: 152 mg
Iron: 4 mg   Sodium: 69 mg   Dietary Fiber: 13 gm

Put on the Barbecue or Light up the Hibachi? Here are Some Ideas...

All recipes assume you have a medium-hot fire going.

Grilled Sweet Onions

(Makes 2 servings)

We acquired this one from a pharmacist in Norway, who lived above the Arctic Circle and insisted on growing his own sweet onions (not a small task in the land of the midnight sun!).

1 sweet onion (Vidalia and Maui, for example)
2 teaspoons soy sauce
1 teaspoon apple juice concentrate
1 teaspoon vegan margarine

Peel and cut onion in half, lengthwise. Cut a thin slice from each end so the halves will lie flat. Cut a slit in the center of each half, and fill with soy sauce, concentrate, and margarine. Place on a grill, slit side up. Allow onion to barbecue about 10-15 minutes, so it is hot, yet still crunchy. Serve hot.

Note: If sweet onions are not available, purchase small white onions. If there's no hot barbecue around, wrap the onions in foil and bake at 425 degrees for about 15 minutes. Extra portions of onions can be chopped and used in soups and sandwiches.

Total Calories Per Serving: 67   Total Fat as % of Daily Value: 3%
Protein: 2 gm   Fat: 2 gm   Carbohydrates: 11 gm   Calcium: 24 mg
Iron: <1 mg   Sodium: 361 mg   Dietary Fiber: 2 gm

Squash on the Barbie

(Makes 2 servings)

Barbecuing concentrates the sweetness of summer squash.

1 Tablespoon olive oil (other oils are okay)
2 Tablespoons balsamic vinegar (other vinegars are okay)
1 minced garlic clove
1 green onion, chopped
1 Tablespoon dried parsley
1 small summer squash or zucchini, cut into slices (about 1 cup)
1 small eggplant, not peeled, cut into slices (about 1 cup)

In a large plastic or glass bowl, combine oil, vinegar, garlic, onion, and parsley. Allow mixture to sit for 10 minutes. Place squash and eggplant in the marinade and allow it to sit for 20 minutes, turning slices at least once. Place squash and eggplant on a hot barbecue, and cook and turn until golden on each side. Brush with extra marinade, if desired. Serve hot or chill for a cold dish.

Note: If no barbecue is available, this dish can be prepared in a 425-degree oven.

Total Calories Per Serving: 94   Total Fat as % of Daily Value: 11%
Protein: 1 gm   Fat: 7 gm   Carbohydrates: 8 gm   Calcium: 22 mg
Iron: 1 mg   Sodium: 7 mg   Dietary Fiber: 2 gm

Pasta-Stuffed Roasted Peppers
(Makes 2 servings)

Start this recipe in the backyard (or the fire escape!) and finish in the kitchen.

2 medium-sized green or red bell peppers
2 teaspoons olive oil
1-1/2 cups cooked pasta
1/8 cup chopped onions
1/3 cup chopped tomatoes
1/3 cup shredded vegan soy cheese or crumbled firm
    tofu
1 teaspoon granulated garlic
1 teaspoon dried oregano
2 Tablespoons chopped almonds or pine nuts

Cut tops off peppers (save these) and coat with olive oil. Place the peppers on a hot barbecue and cook and turn until the peppers begin to blister (but not blacken). Remove from grill.

In a medium-sized bowl, mix remaining ingredients. Pack filling into peppers and cover with pepper tops. Wrap each pepper tightly in foil and return to the grill to cook (they will steam) for approximately 15 minutes or until hot.

Note: If a barbecue is not available, peppers can be roasted in the direct flame of the stovetop or baked in a 375-degree oven.

Total Calories Per Serving Using Tofu And Pine Nuts: 267
Total Fat as % of Daily Value: 21%
Protein: 13 gm   Fat: 13 gm   Carbohydrates: 29 gm   Calcium: 101 mg
Iron: 7 mg   Sodium: 54 mg   Dietary Fiber: 5 gm

Toasty Brown Gravy

(Makes approximately 1 cup or 8 servings)

Whip up this fast gravy while the vegetables are grilling. Great on grilled veggies, any type of savory tofu, seitan, tempeh, fake meat, or baked or mashed potatoes.

1/4 cup flour
1/2 cup nutritional yeast (for example, Red Star Vegetarian Support Formula)
1/3 cup oil or melted vegan margarine
2 teaspoons soy sauce
1/2 teaspoon black pepper
Hot water as needed

In a small frying pan, toast flour and yeast over high heat until mixture starts to brown and develops a toasty aroma (approximately 4 minutes). Stirring vigorously, add the oil, soy sauce, and pepper to make a smooth paste. Slowly add water, stirring, until you arrive at the gravy consistency you like. Cook for 2 minutes or until thoroughly heated. Serve hot.

Total Calories Per Serving Using Olive Oil: 119
Total Fat as % of Daily Value: 14%
Protein: 5 gm   Fat: 9 gm   Carbohydrates: 6 gm   Calcium: 1 mg
Iron: 1 mg   Sodium: 86 mg   Dietary Fiber: 2 gm

Grilled Corn on the Cob, Curry Style
(Makes 3 ears or 3 servings)

This dish is so luscious! You'll never eat plain corn on the cob again.

3 ears unhusked corn on the cob
3 Tablespoons unsweetened coconut milk
3 teaspoons chopped fresh cilantro (or fresh parsley)
3 teaspoons curry powder
1 teaspoon red pepper flakes

Peel back the husks from the corn and remove the silk (but keep the husks intact). In a small bowl, combine remaining ingredients. Brush mixture on the corn and pull husks back over the corn, so kernels are covered. If husks won't stay, use thin strips of foil as closures. Place the corn on the grill, turning frequently for approximately 15 minutes or until the husks have dried out and the kernels begin to brown.

Note: If there's no barbecue grill available, you can use the same technique in a 475-degree oven.

Total Calories Per Serving: 90   Total Fat as % of Daily Value: 2%
Protein: 3 gm   Fat: 2gm   Carbohydrates: 19 gm   Calcium: 17 mg
Iron: 1 mg   Sodium: 22 mg   Dietary Fiber: 4 gm

Grilled Asparagus
(Makes approximately 4 servings)

*Asparagus is heartier than you think. This dish is a nice altern-
ative to steaming asparagus (you'll need fresh asparagus; frozen
won't yield the right texture).*

**1 pound trimmed fresh asparagus (snap off the first 1/2-
inch of the end)**
1/4 cup oil
1 teaspoon black pepper
2 Tablespoons chopped fresh parsley
1 teaspoon granulated garlic
1 Tablespoon chopped onion

On a plate or baking sheet, roll asparagus in oil. In a small bowl,
mix remaining ingredients. Grill vegetables for approximately 5
minutes, turning once or twice, until asparagus is tender. Remove from grill, place on plate, and sprinkle with oil mixture.

Note: If no barbecue is available, try this recipe in a 475-degree
oven. Put the asparagus on a baking sheet. Try green, white, or
purple asparagus or a new veggie, broccolini (which looks like
asparagus, but is a cross between broccoli rabe and Swiss
chard).

Total Calories Per Serving: 149   Total Fat as % of Daily Value: 21%
Protein: 4 gm   Fat: 14 gm   Carbohydrates: 5 gm   Calcium: 31 mg
Iron: 1 mg   Sodium: 4 mg   Dietary Fiber: 1 gm

Grilled Veggie Sub

(Makes 3 servings)

Grill some extra veggies and make a wonderful lunch the next day.

1/2 cup red onion wedges
1/4 cup green peppers, cut into strips
1/4 cup red peppers, cut into strips
1 cup thinly sliced eggplant
1 cup thinly sliced zucchini
1 Tablespoon granulated garlic
1 Tablespoon dried oregano
2 Tablespoon oil
3 large submarine or hoagie rolls
Shredded lettuce and tomato slices, if desired

Arrange veggies on the barbecue. In a small bowl, mix garlic, oregano, and oil. Brush mixture on veggies. Turn once, brush again, and allow veggies to grill until they achieve the tenderness you desire. Arrange veggies on the rolls. Top with lettuce and tomatoes and eat hot!

Total Calories Per Serving (minus lettuce and tomatoes): 317
Total Fat as % of Daily Value: 21%
Protein: 9 gm   Fat: 14gm   Carbohydrates: 41 gm   Calcium: 121 mg
Iron: 2 mg   Sodium: 344 mg   Dietary Fiber: 5 gm

Glossary

The following definitions are included to assist you in shopping and preparing recipes. Some give more information about vegan products while others offer details on less common cooking terms or products.

Almond Milk: a beverage produced by expressing (pressing) almonds for their liquid. Look for almond milks that are fortified with vitamin A, vitamin D, and calcium. Can be used in most recipes that call for soy or rice milk.

Balsamic Vinegar: vinegar that has been aged in oak barrels. Balsamic can be aged anywhere from one month to several years. It is thought to have originated in Modena, Italy. Some of the best balsamic still is exported from there. Balsamic vinegar is deep red, almost syrup-like in consistency, and has a complex flavor.

Dry Sweetener: some vegans use refined white sugar and some choose not to use it. Cane sugar is processed often with filtration equipment that contains animal products (bone char). Some cane refineries, such as the producers of Jack Frost Sugar, do not use bone char. Neither does the manufacturer of Florida Crystal Sugar. Beet sugar refineries never use a bone char filter. Beet sugar is often labeled Granulated Sugar. There are many alternate products on the market, such as dried cane sugar (one of the brand names is Succanat), dried maple sugar, and turbinado sugar. Try out the various types and see which works best for you in terms of taste and texture. For this book, wherever you see "dry sweetener" listed as an ingredient, you may use sucrose (white sugar) or any vegan dry sweetening product. Please don't substitute liquid sweeteners, as they will not yield the right texture in the recipes. Artificial sweeteners, such as saccharin, will not work in these recipes. Stevia, a naturally derived sweetener, is too concentrated for cooking recipes (and at the time of this writing, is very expensive).

Edamame: the Japanese name for fresh soybeans. Before they are dried, soybeans are green. These can be steamed for a snack or used as an addition for soups, salads, casseroles, etc. May be available fresh at farmers' markets or Asian markets; are available frozen in many grocery stores.

Liquid Sweeteners: many vegans, in addition to avoiding white sugar, also don't use honey. Alternate types of sweeteners are dry sweeteners (explained above) and syrups, such as rice syrup, malt syrup, and maple syrup. Puréed fruit, thawed orange juice and apple juice concentrate, applesauce, and fruit butters (such as apple butter) are also used for sweetening.

Measurements: just to refresh your memory
3 teaspoons = 1 Tablespoon
2 Tablespoons = 1 ounce
1 cup = 8 ounces
1/8 cup = 1 ounce or 2 Tablespoons
1/4 cup = 2 ounces or 4 Tablespoons
1/2 cup = 4 ounces
3/4 cup = 6 ounces
1 pint = 2 cups or 16 ounces
1 quart = 4 cups or 32 ounces
1 pound = 16 ounces

Nonreactive: when you are cooking, you don't want the material of the container to react with the ingredients. This may cause discoloring of the food or effect its taste. An example would be heating soymilk in an aluminum pan; the milk will turn gray. Plastic and glass, where cooking is concerned, are nonreactive materials.

Nut Butters: go beyond peanut butter. Nut butters are made from soybeans, almonds, hazelnuts, and pistachios, to name a few. Use as a sandwich spread, as a dessert topping, and as an ingredient in baking.

Nutritional Yeast: nutritional yeast sometimes is fortified with vitamin B12. Red Star Company makes a "Vegetarian Support Formula" nutritional yeast which contains vitamin B12. This is a good source of B12 for vegans. Read the labels. Not all nutritional yeasts contain vitamin B12 and some are not vegan (they may contain whey). You can sprinkle nutritional yeast on hot or cold cereal, on soups, in baking batters and doughs, on cooked veggies, and in casseroles. We recommend avoiding amino acid preparations.

Pareve: a kosher designation found on food labels. According to kosher tradition, pareve foods are "neutral." This does not help when looking for vegan products, as pareve foods are allowed to contain eggs and fish.

Prepared Mustard: when you see this in a recipe, it means the mustard that comes ready to use (you know, the stuff you smear on your veggie hot dog at the ball game). This is opposed to dry mustard, which is a powder that you keep on your spice rack. Prepared mustard is a blend of ground mustard seeds, vinegar, turmeric (actually a natural color, called "poor man's saffron"), and white pepper. Dry mustard is simply ground mustard seeds. It is important, when following a recipe, to use the form of mustard specified.

Rice Milk: a beverage made by cooking and processing rice to manufacture a milky liquid. Look for rice milks that are fortified with calcium, vitamin A, and vitamin D. Can be used when soy, grain, or nut milks are called for in a recipe.

Seitan: is also called "meat of the wheat." Made by extracting the gluten, or main protein, from wheat, seitan is chewy and stands up well to heat. Can be grilled as a "steak" or cut into pieces and stir-fried or baked. You can purchase seitan already made or make your own from seitan mixes.

Soy Cheeses: read the label. Be sure that the "vegetarian cheese" (as they are often billed) does not contain lactose, milk solids, casein, whey, or rennet. If the package lists "enzymes," you may want to write to the company to be sure the enzymes are of plant or chemical origin.

Soy Crumbles: there are several frozen products that are sold as "soy crumbles." What we are looking for is sausage-style, small pieces of soy (or tempeh or seitan) that can be used to add texture and flavor to recipes. If you can't find soy crumbles, make your own by crumbling soy sausage or breakfast strips or slicing veggie hot dogs. We generally find them in the frozen section, with the breakfast items.

Soy Mayonnaise: you can purchase vegan soy mayonnaise or make your own. If you make your own, be sure to keep it tightly covered, stored in the refrigerator, and discard after 5 days. To make 1-1/2 cups of soy mayonnaise, drain 12-ounces firm tofu. Place in blender and blend on high for 1 minute. Add 2 Tablespoons lemon juice, 2 Tablespoons rice syrup or other liquid sweetener, 2 teaspoons white vinegar, 1 teaspoon prepared mustard, and 1 teaspoon nutritional yeast (optional, but very good for you). Blend until smooth. Cover and refrigerate. It may need to be stirred before each use.

Total Calories Per 2 Tablespoon Serving: 50
Total Fat as % of Daily Value: 4%
Protein: 5 gm   Fat: 3 gm   Carbohydrates: 4 gm   Calcium: 49 mg
Iron: 3 mg   Sodium: 10 mg   Dietary Fiber: 1 gm

Soymilk: the step before tofu! Soybeans are cooked and pressed for their liquid. Soymilk is available in different percentages of fat and in various flavors. Look for soymilks that are fortified with calcium, vitamin A, and vitamin D.

Soy Sour Cream: you can purchase soy sour cream or prepare your own. Simply purée 1 cup of silken tofu with 2 Tablespoons lemon juice in a blender until smooth. Cover and store in the refrigerator. Serves 8 and will last approximately 3 days.

Total Calories Per Serving: 18   Total Fat as % of Daily Value: 1%
Protein: 2 gm   Fat: 1 gm   Carbohydrates: 1 gm   Calcium: 10 mg
Iron: <1 mg   Sodium: 2 mg   Dietary Fiber: <1 gm

Soy Substitutes: if you'd like to veganize some of your old recipes, the following chart should be helpful:

Dairy or Meat	Soy Substitute
1 cup ricotta cheese	1 cup mashed firm tofu
1 cup milk	1 cup soy, rice, grain, or almond milk
1 large egg	2 Tablespoons puréed firm tofu
1 cup yogurt	1 cup soy yogurt or 1 cup puréed silken tofu with 1 Tablespoon lemon juice
1 cup sour cream	1 cup commercial soy sour cream or see recipe above
1 ounce milk chocolate (for baking)	3 ounces (6 Tablespoons) unsweetened cocoa powder with 1 Tablespoon vegetable oil
1 pound ground beef (for sauces, etc.)	1 pound cubed firm tofu or 12 ounces (1-1/2 cups) crumbled seitan or tempeh
1 cup ice cream	1 cup sorbet or soy or rice ice cream

Tempeh: is fermented soy protein. It has a nutty, smoky taste, and a chewier, firmer texture than tofu. Use it on the grill, in the oven, or for stovetop sautéing. Tempeh is available in various flavors.

Tofu: all tofu is made from pressed soybeans. Some tofu is processed with calcium (see Chapter 2 for more discussion on calcium), which can be a vegan calcium source. You can purchase fresh tofu, which needs refrigeration, or aseptically packaged tofu, which does not need refrigeration until the package is opened. There are different textures and flavors of tofu. Tofu is already cooked, so you can take it out of the package and mix it with veggies and salsa or fruit and preserves. Remember that tofu is relatively bland and will take on any flavor you give it. Firm tofu will hold its shape well. Cut it into cubes and toss it into salads, stir-fry or sauté it, or bake it. Silken or soft tofu can be blended for sauces, soups, smoothies, and salad dressings. Remember to refrigerate tofu, as it is perishable.

Vegan Filled Pasta: many pastas are filled, such as ravioli, tortellini, and gnocchi. Read the labels to be sure they are vegan (for example, do not contain eggs or cheese). They are often stuffed with veggies, herbs, potato, or soy products.

Vegan Tortillas: some flour tortillas may be made with lard, so read the labels and get to know the brands.

Vegetable Broth: used instead of chicken or meat broth. Make up a batch and freeze it to use as needed. The following recipe makes about 1 quart:

- 1 teaspoon oil
- 1/2 cup chopped onions
- 1/4 cup chopped celery
- 1/4 cup chopped carrots
- 1/2 cup peeled, diced sweet potatoes
- 1/2 cup peeled, diced turnips or parsnips
- 2 minced garlic cloves
- 1 teaspoon dried thyme
- 1 bay leaf
- 1 quart water
- 1/2 teaspoon black pepper
- 1/4 cup minced fresh dill

Heat oil in a large pot and add onions, celery, carrots, sweet potatoes, turnips, garlic, and thyme. Cook until browned. Add bay leaf and water and bring to a quick boil. Reduce heat, cover, and allow broth to simmer until vegetables are very tender, approximately 35 minutes. Add pepper and dill and cook for 2 minutes. Remove from heat. If desired, broth can be strained and the vegetables used for soups or stews.

Total Calories Per Recipe: 193   Total Fat as % of Daily Value: 8%
Protein: 4 gm   Fat: 5 gm   Carbohydrates: 35 gm   Calcium: 122 mg
Iron: 4 mg   Sodium: 94 mg   Dietary Fiber: 7 gm

Vegetarian Versus Vegan Products: vegetarian products may contain eggs, cheese, dairy, or honey. Vegan products should not contain any animal products. Read the label!

Resources from The Vegetarian Resource Group

The following resources can be purchased from The Vegetarian Resource Group, PO Box 1463, Baltimore, MD 21203. You can order online at <www.vrg.org> or charge your order over the phone by calling (410) 366-8343 between 9am and 5pm EST Monday-Friday.

Please note that the price given includes postage (surface rate) in the United States. If you want your order sent via FedEx Ground please add $4 to your order. Also, outside the USA please pay in US funds by VISA or MasterCard or US dollar money order and add $3 per book for postage.

VEGAN HANDBOOK
Edited by Debra Wasserman & Reed Mangels, Ph.D., R.D.

Over 200 vegan recipes including the basics, international cuisine, and gourmet dishes can be found in this book. Also includes sports nutrition, a seniors' guide to good nutrition, dietary exchange lists for meal planning, online resources, feeding vegan kids, vegetarian history, and much more. The book is 256 pages. TRADE PAPERBACK, $20

SIMPLY VEGAN
Quick Vegetarian Meals, 3rd Edition
By Debra Wasserman & Reed Mangels, Ph.D., R.D.

Simply Vegan is an easy-to-use vegetarian guide that contains over 160 kitchen-tested vegan recipes (no meat, fish, fowl, dairy, or eggs). Each recipe is accompanied by a nutritional analysis.

Reed Mangels, Ph.D., R.D., has included an extensive vegan nutrition section on topics such as Protein, Fat, Calcium, Iron, Vitamin B12, Pregnancy and the Vegan Diet, Feeding Vegan Children, and Calories, Weight Gain, and Weight Loss. A Nutrition Glossary is provided, along with sample menus, meal plans, and a list of the top recipes for Iron, Calcium, and Vitamin C.

Also featured are food definitions and origins, and a comprehensive list of mail-order companies that specialize in selling vegan food, natural clothing, cruelty-free cosmetics, and ecologically-based household products. TRADE PAPERBACK $13

NO CHOLESTEROL PASSOVER RECIPES
100 Vegan Recipes
By Debra Wasserman & Charles Stahler

For many, low-calorie Passover recipes are quite a challenge. Here is a wonderful collection of Passover dishes that are non-dairy, no-cholesterol, eggless, and vegetarian. It includes recipes for eggless blintzes, dairyless carrot cream soup, festive macaroons, apple latkes, sweet and sour cabbage, knishes, broccoli with almond sauce, mock "chopped liver," no oil lemon dressing, eggless matzo meal pancakes, and much more. TRADE PAPERBACK $9

THE LOWFAT JEWISH VEGETARIAN COOKBOOK
Healthy Traditions from Around The World
By Debra Wasserman

The Lowfat Jewish Vegetarian Cookbook contains over 150 lowfat, vegan international recipes. Savor potato knishes, Polish plum and rhubarb soup, Indian curry and rice, Greek pastries, and spinach pies. Feast on Romanian apricot dumplings, North African barley pudding, pumpernickel and Russian flat bread, sweet fruit kugel, Czechoslovakian noodles with poppy seeds, and Russian blini. Celebrate with eggless challah, hamentashen for Purim, Chanukah latkes, mock "chopped liver," Russian charoset, eggless matzo balls, and Syrian wheat pudding.

Breakfast, lunch, and dinner menus are provided, as well as 33 unique Passover dishes and Seder ideas, and Rosh Hashanah Dinner suggestions. Each recipe is accompanied by a nutritional analysis. TRADE PAPERBACK $15

VEGETARIAN QUANTITY RECIPES
From The Vegetarian Resource Group

Here is a helpful kit for people who must cook for large groups and institutional settings. It contains 28 vegan recipes including main dishes, burgers, sandwich spreads, side dishes, soups, salads, desserts, and breakfast. Each recipe provides a serving for 25 and 50 people, and a nutritional analysis. The kit also contains a listing of over 140 companies offering vegetarian food items in institutional sizes and "Tips for Introducing Vegetarian Food into Institutions." PACKET $15

MEATLESS MEALS FOR WORKING PEOPLE
Quick and Easy Vegetarian Recipes, 3rd Edition
By Debra Wasserman & Charles Stahler

Vegetarian cooking can be simple or complicated. The Vegetarian Resource Group recommends using whole grains and fresh vegetables whenever possible. For the busy working person, this isn't always possible. Meatless Meals For Working People contains over 100 delicious fast and easy recipes, plus ideas which teach you how to be a vegetarian within your hectic schedule using common convenient vegetarian foods. This 192-page handy guide also contains a spice chart, party ideas, information on quick service restaurant chains, and much more. TRADE PAPERBACK $12

VEGAN IN VOLUME
Vegan Quantity Recipes for Every Occasion
By Chef Nancy Berkoff, R.D.

This 272-page book has 125 quantity recipes for every occasion. Chef Nancy Berkoff offers help with catered events, weddings, birthdays, college food service, hospital meals, restaurants, dinner parties, and more. She shares her knowledge of vegan nutrition, vegan ingredients, menus for seniors, breakfast buffets, desserts, cooking for kids, and more. TRADE PAPERBACK $20

VEGETARIAN JOURNAL'S FOODSERVICE UPDATE NEWSLETTER
Edited by The Vegetarian Resource Group staff

This quarterly newsletter is for food service personnel and others working for healthier food in schools, restaurants, hospitals, and other institutions. *Vegetarian Journal's Foodservice Update* offers advice, shares quantity recipes, and spotlights leaders in the industry who are providing the healthy options being looked for by consumers. NEWSLETTER $30 includes both Vegetarian Journal and Vegetarian Journal's Foodservice Update in the USA. Inquire about foreign rates.

VEGETARIAN JOURNAL'S GUIDE TO NATURAL FOODS RESTAURANTS IN THE U.S. & CANADA
Edited by The Vegetarian Resource Group

For the health-conscious traveler, this is the perfect traveling companion to insure a great meal or the ideal lodgings when away from home or if you are looking for a nearby vegetarian place. There has been a delightful proliferation of restaurants designed to meet the growing demand for healthier meals. To help locate these places, there is now a single source for information on over 2,000 restaurants, vacation resorts, and more.

The Vegetarian Journal's Guide to Natural Foods Restaurants is a helpful guide listing eateries state by state and province by province. Each entry not only describes the house specialties, varieties of cuisine, and special dietary menus, but also includes information on ambiance, attire, and reservations. It even tells you whether or not you can pay by credit card. And there's more. Included in this guide are listings of vegetarian inns, spas, camps, tours, travel agencies, and vacation spots. TRADE PAPERBACK $16

LEPRECHAUN CAKE AND OTHER TALES
A Vegetarian Story-Cookbook
By Vonnie Winslow Crist and Debra Wasserman

This vegan story-cookbook is for children ages 8 through 11. The book includes a glossary of cooking terms, cleanup and preparation instructions, and safety tips. Children will love preparing and eating the delicious recipes. A leprechaun in the kitchen, a baby dragon down the block, friendly forest deer from South America, and the Snow Queen's Unicorn teach children and adults who love them, about friendship, caring, and healthy cooking. TRADE PAPERBACK $11

FOOD INGREDIENT GUIDE

The Guide to Food Ingredients is a 28-page reference to over 200 mysterious ingredients found on food labels. What makes this food ingredients dictionary unique is that it lists the commercial source for each ingredient. You can quickly determine whether various ingredients are vegetarian, vegan, or neither. For example, did you know that carmine is a food coloring derived from beetles? Also, carrageenan is a seaweed product, which is a common jelling agent. HANDOUT $4

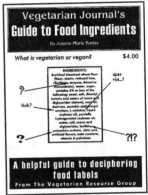

GUIDE TO FAST FOOD

The Guide to Fast Food is a 32-page reference to vegetarian and vegan menu items available at 80 restaurant and quick service chains. It also points out non-vegetarian items, such as fries made with beef fat, chicken broth in sauces, and gelatin in unexpected places. HANDOUT $4

VEGAN & VEGETARIAN FAQ
Answers to Your Frequently Asked Questions
By Davida Gypsy Breier and Reed Mangels, Ph.D., R.D.

Most of us are never going to become vegetarian nutrition experts, but it is likely that we will crave a donut. That's where this 272-page guide to the daily aspects of being a vegetarian is indispensable. Based on answers given to some of the 100,000 visitors to VRG's website (www.vrg.org) every month, this guide addresses the many circumstances of living as a vegetarian.

Oh, and even nutrition experts crave donuts from time to time.

This guide will help non-vegetarians understand some of the issues and ingredients that concern vegetarians. It is also a wonderful starting place if you are a new vegetarian. And if you are a vegetarian 24 hours a day, 7 days a week, you need this book! Vegan & Vegetarian FAQ will make being a vegetarian even easier.

You will find hundreds of answers on everything from vegan marshmallows to food ingredients to veggie kids to how to cook tofu. We've also included 35 popular recipes, including fajitas, sloppy Joes, and eggless banana pancakes, as well as sources for thousands more! TRADE PAPERBACK $15

To order additional copies of
VEGAN MEALS
FOR 1 OR 2
send $15 per book (add $4 for FedEx Ground delivery)
to The Vegetarian Resource Group,
PO Box 1463, Baltimore, MD 21203.
(Outside the USA, pay in US funds only
and add $3 per book for additional postage.)

Join The Vegetarian Resource Group Today and Receive the Bi-Monthly Vegetarian Journal.

Send $20.00 to The Vegetarian Resource Group, P.O. Box 1463, Baltimore, MD 21203. (Mexico/Canada send $32 and other foreign countries send $42 in US funds only.) Orders can be charged over the phone by calling (410) 366-8343 9 am to 6 pm EST or faxed by calling (410) 366-8804.

You can also join online at <www.vrg.org>.

WHAT IS THE VEGETARIAN RESOURCE GROUP?

Our health professionals, activists, and educators work with businesses and individuals to bring about healthy changes in your school, workplace, and community. Registered dietitians and physicians aid in the development of practical nutrition related publications and answer member or media questions about the vegetarian lifestyle.

Vegetarian Journal is one of the benefits members enjoy. Readers receive practical tips for vegetarian meal planning, articles on vegetarian nutrition, recipes, natural food product reviews, and an opportunity to share ideas with others. All nutrition articles are reviewed by a registered dietitian or medical doctor.

The Vegetarian Resource Group also publishes books and special interest newsletters such as Vegetarian Journal's Foodservice Update and Tips for Vegetarian Activists.

Index by Subject

A Place for Everything and Everything in its Place, 19-20
About the Recipes, 15
Barbecue Recipes, Every Day and Special Day, 181-187
Beverages, 54-55 and 128-139
Breakfast, 25 and 34-55
Breakfast Items to Have on Hand, 35
Breakfast Recipes, 38-55
Calcium, 10
Cold Beverages, Grab-and-Go, 133-139
Definitions, 188-194
Desserts, 140-152
Dinner, 25
Entrées, Every Day and Special Day, 166-180
Entrées, Grab-and-Go, 118-127
Every Day and Special Day Cooking, 163
Fast Breakfast Ideas to Get You Started, 37
Fat, 11
Freeze or Refrigerate Now, Eat Later, 86
Fruit, 24
Glossary, 188-194
Grab-and-Go, 113
Grains, 23
Healthy Living, 13
Hot Beverages, Grab-and-Go, 128-132
Index by Major Ingredients, 207-216
Index by Subject, 203
Index to Recipes, 204-207
Iron, 10
Items to Have on Hand, 35-37
It's all about You!, 8
Join The Vegetarian Resource Group, 202
Leftover Creations, 114

Less Common Cooking Terms or Products, 188-194
Lunch, 25
Kitchen Safety, 32
Make Now Use for the Week, 100
Meal Planning and Shopping, 22
Measurements, 189
Menu, Sample, 25-26
Nonreactive, 189
Nutrition, Vegan, 9
One-Pot Wonders, 56-85
Pareve, 190
Pizza-Combination Ideas, 89
Preface, 7
Preparing Meals for One or Two, 21
Protein, 9 and 23
Quick Leftover Combinations, 114-115
Sample Menu, 25-26
Several Words about Purchasing Ingredients, 17
Shopping and Stocking, 26-31
Snacks, 26 and 153-162
Soy Substitutes, 192
Stocking the Shelves, 18
Table of Contents, 5-6
Tools of the Trade, 31
Variations of Veggie Burger Grab, 121
Vegan Meal Planning, 23-24
Vegan Nutrition, 9
Vegetarian Journal, 202
Vegetarian Resource Group Books, The, 195-201
Vegetarian Resource Group, What is The, 202
Vegetarian Versus Vegan Products, 194
Veggies, 24
Vitamin B12, 11
Vitamin C, 10
Why this Book?, 8

Index to Recipes

BARBECUE DISHES
Grilled Asparagus, 186
Grilled Corn on the Cob, Curry Style, 185
Grilled Sweet Onions, 181
Grilled Veggie Sub, 187
Pasta-Stuffed Roasted Peppers, 183
Squash on the Barbie, 182

BEVERAGES (See Grab-and-Go Hot Beverages and Grab-and-Go Cold Beverages)

BREAKFASTS
Apple Oatmeal, 46
Apple Yogurt, 46
Breakfast Potato Burritos, 43
Breakfast Snaps, 52
Breakfast Stacks, 53
Chocolate-on-the-Run, 54
Cinnamon and Potato Pancakes, 41
Cinnamon, Apple, and Raisin Pancakes, 40
Corny French Toast, 39
Creamy Baked Fruit Gratin, 50
Fruit Granola, 49
Ginger-Molasses Crunch, 48
Hot Apples and Sweet Potatoes, 51
Latin A.M. Chocolate, 55
Macadamia Nut Pancakes, 42
Revved-Up Oatmeal, 45
Tofu Scramble, 38
Upside-Down Pecan-Bran Muffins, 44
Your Own Granola, 47

DESSERTS
Almond Rice Pudding, 150
Baked Pears in Apple Cider Syrup, 142
Chocolate Dream, 146
Cool and Smooth Fruit, 145
Crock Pot Cherry Cobbler, 149
Frozen Berry Banana "Ice Cream," 151
Frozen Tropicale, 152
Fruit and Graham Crisp, 148
Ginger and Wine Marinated Fruit, 111
Graham Pudding Parfaits, 147
Hot Spicy Fruit Stew, 112
Pear Pie, 143
Pears in Parchment, 144

DRESSINGS
Garlicky Caesar Dressing, 103
Green and Creamy Dressing, 104
Orange Tahini Dressing, 105
Peanut and Onion Dressing, 101
Roasted Garlic and Basil Spread, 107
Tomato-Mustard Vinaigrette, 102

ENTRÉES (Also see Grab-and-Go Entrées)
Almost Thai Spicy Peanut Pasta, 170
Asian Sautéed Eggplant, 177
Better Than Beef Stew, 94
Cauliflower Curry, 84
Comfort Casserole (Baked Pasta and Peppers), 69
Confetti Pasta, 169
Crank Up the Heat Rice and Beans, 73
Dahl, 91
Drunken Carrots with Tofu, 178
Freezer Pizza, 88
Hoppin' John, 76
Is it Tofu? Is it Tempeh? It's Garlic, For Sure, 85

Italian Tofu with Mushrooms and Peppers, 167
Lentil-Spinach Pilaf, 74
Mediterranean Stuffed Veggies, 176
Multi-Colored Pasta with Broccoli, 166
Pasta in Paradise, 67
Pasta Now, Pasta Later, 68
Pasta with Sun-Dried Tomatoes and Wild Mushrooms, 168
Peanut-Tofu Stew, 175
Potato Tacos, 172
Power Chili, 95
Put Together in Ten Minutes Casserole, 77
Quick Cajun Rice and Beans, 81
Quick Tofu Stroganoff, 179
Red Pepper and Pine Nut Orzo, 171
Red Potato, Mustard Green, and Mushroom Sauté, 173
Smoky Black Beans, 90
Stuffed Peppers, 93
Tofu (or Seitan or Tempeh) Aztec, 174
Upscale Greens with Avocado and Chilies, 180
Vegetables Provencale, 96
Zucchini, Green Bean, and Potato Stew, 83

GRAB-AND-GO COLD BEVERAGES

Banana-Blueberry Smoothie, 136
Chocolate-Covered Cherry Smoothie, 134
Gingered Lemon, Lime, or Orange-ade, 138
Mango Lemonade, 139
Mint Chocolate Peanut Butter Re-fresher, 135
Mongo Mango Smoothie, 136
Orange Swirl, 133
Pineapple Smoothie, 137
Raspberries and Cream Smoothie, 134
Watermelon Lemonade, 138

GRAB-AND-GO ENTRÉES

Baked Beans Quesadillas, 124
Garbanzo-Spinach Curry, 126
Green and Crunchy Salad, 118
Lemon Tofu and Spinach Bake, 123
Oktoberfest Kraut and Beans, 125
One Dish Potato Bar, 127
Speedy Tostadas, 122
Spur of the Moment Salad, 119
Veggie Burger Grab, 120

GRAB-AND-GO HOT BEVERAGES

Almond Latte, 128
Chocolate-on-the-Run, 54
Citrus Fruit Tea, 131
Gingery Tea, 131
Latin A.M. Chocolate, 55
Lemonade Tea, 130
Orange Chocolate Latte, 130
Peppermint Chocolate Latte, 129
Rainy Day Tea, 132

ONE-POT MEALS

Asian Cabbage and Green Onions, 82
Asian Noodle Bowl, 66
Cauliflower Curry, 84
Cool-As-A-Cucumber Soup, 61
Comfort Casserole (Baked Pasta and Peppers), 69
Corn and Potato Chowder, 60
Crank Up the Heat Rice and Beans, 73
Cucumber Raita, 65
Garbs and Carbs, 75
Garlic and Rosemary Sweet Pota-toes, 71
Hoppin' John, 76
Is it Tofu? Is it Tempeh? It's Garlic, For Sure, 85
Kitchen Sink Minestrone, 59
Lentil-Spinach Pilaf, 74
Pasta in Paradise, 67
Pasta Now, Pasta Later, 68

Put Together in Ten Minutes Casserole, 77

Quick Cajun Rice and Beans, 81

Raisins and Brown Rice, 78

Salsa Black Bean Salad, 63

Spicy Pepper-Corn and Coconut Milk, 72

Sufferin' Sweet Potato Succotash, 70

Sweet Indian Rice with Carrots and Dates, 79

Tangy Tofu Salad, 64

Wild Rice Pilaf with Celery and Carrots, 80

Wonder Gazpacho, 62

Zucchini, Green Bean, and Potato Stew, 83

RECIPES YOU CAN FREEZE

Balsamic Tomato Soup or Sauce, 98

Beet and Dill Pancakes, 92

Better Than Beef Stew, 94

Creamy Carrot Soup, 99

Dahl, 91

Freezer Pizza, 88

Green and Creamy Soup, 97

Power Chili, 95

Smoky Black Beans, 90

Stuffed Peppers, 93

Vegetables Provencale, 96

RECIPES YOU CAN REFRIGERATE

Garlic Soup/Sauce, 110

Garlicky Caesar Dressing, 103

Ginger and Wine Marinated Fruit, 111

Green and Creamy Dressing, 104

Hot Spicy Fruit Stew, 112

Low Fat Raspberry Marinade, 106

Orange Tahini Dressing, 105

Peanut and Onion Dressing, 101

Peperonata, 108

Pepper Blast, 109

Roasted Garlic and Basil Spread, 107

Tomato-Mustard Vinaigrette, 102

SALADS

Garbs and Carbs, 75

Green and Crunchy Salad, 118

Salsa Black Bean Salad, 63

Spur of the Moment Salad, 119

Tangy Tofu Salad, 64

Upscale Greens with Avocado and Chilies, 180

SAUCES, MARINADES, OR GRAVY

Balsamic Tomato Soup or Sauce, 98

Garlic Soup/Sauce, 110

Low Fat Raspberry Marinade, 106

Peperonata, 108

Soy Mayonnaise, 191

Toasty Brown Gravy, 184

SIDE DISHES

Asian Cabbage and Green Onions, 82

Beet and Dill Pancakes, 92

Cucumber Raita, 65

Garlic and Rosemary Sweet Potatoes, 71

Raisins and Brown Rice, 78

Spicy Pepper-Corn and Coconut Milk, 72

Sufferin' Sweet Potato Succotash, 70

Sweet Indian Rice with Carrots and Dates, 79

Wild Rice Pilaf with Celery and Carrots, 80

SNACKS

Baked Veggie Chips, 158
Brochettes, 162
Carrot Orange Cookies, 154
Chili Snack Crunch, 161
Crackers and Herbs, 160
Mediterranean Artichoke Nibblers, 159
Peanut Butter-Graham Roundies, 155
Pineapple and Baked Beans Dip, 157
Striped Parfait, 156
Your Own Personal Power Bar, 153

SOUPS

Asian Noodle Bowl, 66
Balsamic Tomato Soup or Sauce, 98
Cool-As-A-Cucumber Soup, 61
Corn and Potato Chowder, 60
Creamy Carrot Soup, 99
Garlic Soup/Sauce, 110
Green and Creamy Soup, 97
Kitchen Sink Minestrone, 59
Peanut and Onion Dressing, 101
Vegetable Broth, 194
Wonder Gazpacho, 62

Index by Major Ingredients

ALMOND MILK (Also see soy or rice milk)
Glossary definition, 188

ALMONDS
Raisins and Brown Rice, 78

APPLE BUTTER
Apple Yogurt, 46

APPLE CIDER
Baked Pears in Apple Cider Syrup, 142

APPLES
Apple Oatmeal, 46
Cinnamon, Apple, and Raisin Pancakes, 40
Hot Apples and Sweet Potatoes, 51

APPLESAUCE
Hot Spicy Fruit Stew, 112

APRICOTS
Hot Spicy Fruit Stew, 112

ARTICHOKE HEARTS
Mediterranean Artichoke Nibblers, 159

ASPARAGUS
Confetti Pasta, 169
Grilled Asparagus, 186

AVOCADO
Upscale Greens with Avocado and Chilies, 180

BAKED BEANS
Baked Beans Quesadillas, 124
Oktoberfest Kraut and Beans, 125
One Dish Potato Bar, 127
Pineapple and Baked Beans Dip, 157

BALSAMIC VINEGAR
Glossary definition, 188

BANANAS
Banana-Blueberry Smoothie, 136
Creamy Baked Fruit Gratin, 50
Frozen Berry Banana "Ice Cream,"
151
Mongo Mango Smoothie, 136
Pineapple Smoothie, 137

BARLEY
Stuffed Peppers, 93

BASIL
Roasted Garlic and Basil Spread,
107

BASMATI RICE (See rice)

BEER, VEGAN
Drunken Carrots with Tofu, 178

BEETS
Baked Veggie Chips, 158
Beet and Dill Pancakes, 92

BERRIES
Cool and Smooth Fruit, 145
Frozen Berry Banana "Ice Cream,"
151
Graham Pudding Parfaits, 147
Striped Parfait, 156

BLACK BEANS
Salsa Black Bean Salad, 63
Smoky Black Beans, 90

BLACK-EYED PEAS
Hoppin' John, 76

BLUEBERRIES (Also see berries)
Banana-Blueberry Smoothie, 136

BREAD
Breakfast Stacks, 53
Corny French Toast, 39

Spur of the Moment Salad, 119

BRAZIL NUTS
Carrot Orange Cookies, 154
Your Own Granola, 47

BROCCOLI
Multi-Colored Pasta with Broccoli,
166

BROWN RICE (See rice)

CABBAGE
Asian Cabbage and Green Onions,
82

CAKE MIX, VEGAN YELLOW
Crock Pot Cherry Cobbler, 149

CAROB CHIPS, VEGAN
Chocolate Dream, 146

CARROT JUICE
Creamy Carrot Soup, 99

CARROTS
Almost Thai Spicy Peanut Pasta, 170
Baked Veggie Chips, 158
Better Than Beef Stew, 94
Carrot Orange Cookies, 154
Creamy Carrot Soup, 99
Drunken Carrots with Tofu, 178
Sweet Indian Rice with Carrots and
Dates, 79
Tofu (or Seitan or Tempeh) Aztec,
174
Wild Rice Pilaf with Celery and
Carrots, 80

CASHEWS
Your Own Granola, 47

CAULIFLOWER
Cauliflower Curry, 84

CELERY
Garbs and Carbs, 75
Put Together in Ten Minutes
  Casserole, 77
Wild Rice Pilaf with Celery and
  Carrots, 80

CEREAL, DRY
Breakfast Snaps, 52
Peanut Butter-Graham Roundies,
  155
Your Own Personal Power Bar, 153

CHERRIES, FROZEN
Chocolate-Covered Cherry
  Smoothie, 134

CHERRY PIE FILLING, VEGAN
Crock Pot Cherry Cobbler, 149

CHICKPEAS (See garbanzo beans)

CHOCOLATE CHIPS, VEGAN
Chocolate Dream, 146

CHOW MEIN NOODLES, VEGAN
Put Together in Ten Minutes
  Casserole, 77

COCOA POWDER
Chocolate-on-the-Run, 54

COCONUT MILK
Cauliflower Curry, 84
Grilled Corn on the Cob, Curry
  Style, 185
Pepper Blast, 109
Spicy Pepper-Corn and Coconut
  Milk, 72

COCONUT, SHREDDED
Your Own Granola, 47

COFFEE
Almond Latte, 128
Orange Chocolate Latte, 130
Peppermint Chocolate Latte, 129

CORN
Corn and Potato Chowder, 60
Grilled Corn on the Cob, Curry Style,
  185
Pasta Now, Pasta Later, 68
Power Chili, 95
Spicy Pepper-Corn and Coconut
  Milk, 72
Sufferin' Sweet Potato Succotash, 70

CORNFLAKES (Also see dry cereal)
Corny French Toast, 39
Your Own Personal Power Bar, 153

CRANBERRIES
Stuffed Peppers, 93

CUCUMBER
Cool-As-A-Cucumber Soup, 61
Cucumber Raita, 65
Garbs and Carbs, 75

DATES
Breakfast Snaps, 52
Sweet Indian Rice with Carrots and
  Dates, 79
Your Own Personal Power Bar, 153

DRIED FRUIT, MIXED
Your Own Granola, 47

DRY SWEETENER
Glossary definition, 188

EDAMAME
Glossary definition, 189

EGGPLANT
Asian Sautéed Eggplant, 177
Grilled Veggie Sub, 187
Peperonata, 108
Squash on the Barbie, 182
Vegetables Provencale, 96

FIGS
Your Own Personal Power Bar, 153

GARBANZO BEANS
Garbanzo-Spinach Curry, 126
Garbs and Carbs, 75

GARLIC
Garbanzo-Spinach Curry, 126
Garlic Soup/Sauce, 110
Garlicky Caesar Dressing, 103
Roasted Garlic and Basil Spread,
   107

GINGER
Gingered Lemon, Lime, or Orange-
   ade, 138
Gingery Tea, 131

GLUTEN, WHEAT (See seitan)

GNOCCHI, VEGAN
Brochettes, 162
Glossary definition, 193

GRAHAM CRACKER CRUMBS, VEGAN
Chocolate Dream, 146
Graham Pudding Parfaits, 147
Peanut Butter-Graham Roundies,
   155
Your Own Personal Power Bar, 153

GRAHAM CRACKERS
Fruit and Graham Crisp, 148

GREEN BEANS
Zucchini, Green Bean, and Potato
   Stew, 83

GREENS (See kale or mustard greens)

GREEN SALAD
Green and Crunchy Salad, 118

HASH BROWN POTATOES
Breakfast Potato Burritos, 43
Cinnamon and Potato Pancakes, 41
Potato Tacos, 172

ICE CREAM, VEGAN
Cool and Smooth Fruit, 145
Crock Pot Cherry Cobbler, 149
Fruit and Graham Crisp, 148
Mint Chocolate Peanut Butter Re-
   fresher, 135
Orange Swirl, 133

KALE
Red Potato, Mustard Green, and
   Mushroom Sauté, 173

KIDNEY BEANS
Crank Up the Heat Rice and Beans,
   73
Kitchen Sink Minestrone, 59
Quick Cajun Rice and Beans, 81

LEMON JUICE
Gingered Lemon, Lime, or Orange-
   ade, 138
Mango Lemonade, 139
Watermelon Lemonade, 138

LENTILS
Dahl, 91
Lentil-Spinach Pilaf, 74

LETTUCE
Upscale Greens with Avocado and
  Chilies, 180

LIMA BEANS
Sufferin' Sweet Potato Succotash,
  70

LIME JUICE
Gingered Lemon, Lime, or Orange-
  ade, 138

LIQUID SWEETENERS
Glossary definition, 189

MACADAMIA NUTS
Macadamia Nut Pancakes, 42

MANGO
Mango Lemonade, 139
Pasta in Paradise, 67

MANGO JUICE
Mongo Mango Smoothie, 136

MAPLE SYRUP
Upside-Down Pecan-Bran Muffins,
  44
Your Own Granola, 47

MELON (Also see watermelon)
Cool and Smooth Fruit, 145

MUSHROOMS
Better Than Beef Stew, 94
Italian Tofu with Mushrooms and
  Peppers, 167
Pasta with Sun-Dried Tomatoes
  and Wild Mushrooms, 168
Quick Tofu Stroganoff, 179
Red Potato, Mustard Green, and
  Mushroom Sauté, 173
Vegetables Provencale, 96

MUSTARD GREENS
Red Potato, Mustard Green, and
  Mushroom Sauté, 173

NOODLES, VEGAN
Asian Noodle Bowl, 66

NUT BUTTERS
Glossary definition, 190

NUTRITIONAL YEAST
Glossary definition, 190
Toasty Brown Gravy, 184

OAT BRAN
Ginger-Molasses Crunch, 48
Upside-Down Pecan-Bran Muffins,
  44

ONIONS
Better Than Beef Stew, 94
Corn and Potato Chowder, 60
Dahl, 91
Green and Creamy Soup, 97
Grilled Sweet Onions, 181
Grilled Veggie Sub, 187
Mediterranean Stuffed Veggies, 176
Peperonata, 108
Power Chili, 95
Quick Cajun Rice and Beans, 81
Quick Tofu Stroganoff, 179
Wild Rice Pilaf with Celery and
  Carrots, 80

ORANGE JUICE
Gingered Lemon, Lime, or Orange-
  ade, 138
Pineapple Smoothie, 137

ORANGES
Orange Tahini Dressing, 105

PAPAYA
Pasta in Paradise, 67

PASTA
Almost Thai Spicy Peanut Pasta, 170
Comfort Casserole (Baked Pasta and Peppers), 69
Confetti Pasta, 169
Multi-Colored Pasta with Broccoli, 166
Pasta in Paradise, 67
Pasta Now, Pasta Later, 68
Pasta-Stuffed Roasted Peppers, 183
Pasta with Sun-Dried Tomatoes and Wild Mushrooms, 168
Red Pepper and Pine Nut Orzo, 171

PEACHES
Hot Spicy Fruit Stew, 112

PEANUT BUTTER
Peanut and Onion Dressing, 101
Peanut Butter-Graham Roundies, 155
Peanut-Tofu Stew, 175

PEARS
Baked Pears in Apple Cider Syrup, 142
Hot Spicy Fruit Stew, 112
Pear Pie, 143
Pears in Parchment, 144

PEAS
Almost Thai Spicy Peanut Pasta, 170

PECANS
Upside-Down Pecan-Bran Muffins, 44
Your Own Granola, 47

PEPPERS, BELL
Italian Tofu with Mushrooms and Peppers, 167
Mediterranean Stuffed Veggies, 176
Pasta Now, Pasta Later, 68
Pasta-Stuffed Roasted Peppers, 183
Peperonata, 108
Quick Cajun Rice and Beans, 81
Red Pepper and Pine Nut Orzo, 171
Stuffed Peppers, 93
Vegetables Provencale, 96

PEPPERS, HOT
Pepper Blast, 109

PINEAPPLE
Frozen Tropicale, 152
Hot Spicy Fruit Stew, 112
Macadamia Nut Pancakes, 42

PINEAPPLE, CANNED CRUSHED
Pineapple and Baked Beans Dip, 157
Pineapple Smoothie, 137

PINE NUTS
Red Pepper and Pine Nut Orzo, 171

POPCORN, VEGAN
Chili Snack Crunch, 161

POTATOES
Baked Veggie Chips, 158
Better Than Beef Stew, 94
Corn and Potato Chowder, 60
One Dish Potato Bar, 127
Red Potato, Mustard Green, and Mushroom Sauté, 173
Tofu (or Seitan or Tempeh) Aztec, 174
Zucchini, Green Bean, and Potato Stew, 83

PREPARED MUSTARD
Glossary definition, 190

PRUNES
Tofu (or Seitan or Tempeh) Aztec, 174
Your Own Personal Power Bar, 153

PUDDING MIX, VEGAN INSTANT
Graham Pudding Parfaits, 147
Striped Parfait, 156

PUMPKIN SEEDS
Your Own Granola, 47

RAISINS
Chili Snack Crunch, 161
Cinnamon, Apple, and Raisin Pancakes, 40
Raisins and Brown Rice, 78
Stuffed Peppers, 93

RASPBERRIES, FROZEN (Also see berries)
Raspberries and Cream Smoothie, 134
Watermelon Lemonade, 138

RAVIOLI, VEGAN
Brochettes, 162
Glossary definition, 193

RED BEANS (See kidney beans)

RICE
Almond Rice Pudding, 150
Crank Up the Heat Rice and Beans, 73
Hoppin' John, 76
Quick Cajun Rice and Beans, 81
Raisins and Brown Rice, 78
Stuffed Peppers, 93
Sweet Indian Rice with Carrots and Dates, 79
Wild Rice Pilaf with Celery and Carrots, 80

RICE MILK (Also see soy or rice milk)
Glossary definition, 190

ROLLED OATS
Apple Oatmeal, 46
Fruit Granola, 49
Ginger-Molasses Crunch, 48
Your Own Granola, 47

SAUERKRAUT
Oktoberfest Kraut and Beans, 125

SEITAN
Asian Noodle Bowl, 66
Better Than Beef Stew, 94
Glossary definition, 191
Hoppin' John, 76
Put Together in Ten Minutes Casserole, 77
Quick Tofu Stroganoff, 179
Tofu (or Seitan or Tempeh) Aztec, 174

SHREDDED WHEAT (Also see dry cereal)
Breakfast Snaps, 52

SORBET, VEGAN
Cool and Smooth Fruit, 145
Crock Pot Cherry Cobbler, 149
Fruit and Graham Crisp, 148
Orange Swirl, 133

SOY CHEESE, VEGAN
Baked Beans Quesadillas, 124
Comfort Casserole (Baked Pasta and Peppers), 69
Glossary definition, 191
Pasta-Stuffed Roasted Peppers, 183
Potato Tacos, 172

SOY CRUMBLES
Breakfast Potato Burritos, 43
Glossary definition, 191
Quick Cajun Rice and Beans, 81

SOY MAYONNAISE
Glossary definition, 191
Soy mayonnaise recipe, 191

SOY OR RICE MILK
Almond Latte, 128
Almond Rice Pudding, 150
Banana-Blueberry Smoothie, 136
Beet and Dill Pancakes, 92
Breakfast Stacks, 53
Chocolate-Covered Cherry Smoothie, 134
Chocolate-on-the-Run, 54
Cinnamon, Apple, and Raisin Pancakes, 40
Corn and Potato Chowder, 60
Creamy Baked Fruit Gratin, 50
Glossary definition, 192
Graham Pudding Parfaits, 147
Is it Tofu? Is it Tempeh? It's Garlic, For Sure, 85
Latin A.M. Chocolate, 55
Mongo Mango Smoothie, 136
Orange Chocolate Latte, 130
Orange Swirl, 133
Peppermint Chocolate Latte, 129
Raspberries and Cream Smoothie, 134
Revved-Up Oatmeal, 45
Striped Parfait, 156
Upside-Down Pecan-Bran Muffins, 44

SOY SOUR CREAM, VEGAN
Brochettes, 162
Comfort Casserole (Baked Pasta and Peppers), 69
Cucumber Raita, 65
Glossary definition, 192
Pasta with Sun-Dried Tomatoes and Wild Mushrooms, 168
Peanut-Tofu Stew, 175
Quick Tofu Stroganoff, 179
Soy sour cream recipe, 192

SOY SAUSAGE
Power Chili, 95
Quick Cajun Rice and Beans, 81
Smoky Black Beans, 90

SOY YOGURT
Apple Yogurt, 46
Cucumber Raita, 65
Frozen Tropicale, 152
Peanut-Tofu Stew, 175

SPINACH
Garbanzo-Spinach Curry, 126
Green and Creamy Soup, 97
Lemon Tofu and Spinach Bake, 123
Lentil-Spinach Pilaf, 74
Mediterranean Stuffed Veggies, 176
Multi-Colored Pasta with Broccoli, 166

SQUASH (See yellow squash)

STRAWBERRIES (Also see berries)
Striped Parfait, 156

SUN-DRIED TOMATOES
Pasta with Sun-Dried Tomatoes and Wild Mushrooms, 168

SUNFLOWER SEEDS
Chili Snack Crunch, 161
Fruit Granola, 49
Your Own Granola, 47

SWEETENERS (See dry sweeteners or liquid sweeteners)

SWEET POTATOES
Garlic and Rosemary Sweet Potatoes, 71
Hot Apples and Sweet Potatoes, 51
Sufferin' Sweet Potato Succotash, 70

TACOS, VEGAN
Potato Tacos, 172

TARO
Baked Veggie Chips, 158

TEA
Citrus Fruit Tea, 131
Lemonade Tea, 130
Rainy Day Tea, 132

TEMPEH
Better Than Beef Stew, 94
Glossary definition, 193
Is it Tofu? Is it Tempeh? It's Garlic,
  For Sure, 85
Potato Tacos, 172
Put Together in Ten Minutes
  Casserole, 77
Quick Tofu Stroganoff, 179
Tofu (or Seitan or Tempeh) Aztec,
  174

TOFU
Asian Noodle Bowl, 66
Chocolate Dream, 146
Corn and Potato Chowder, 60
Creamy Carrot Soup, 99
Drunken Carrots with Tofu, 178
Glossary definition, 193
Green and Creamy Dressing, 104
Hoppin' John, 76
Is it Tofu? Is it Tempeh? It's Garlic,
  For Sure, 85
Italian Tofu with Mushrooms and
  Peppers, 167
Lemon Tofu and Spinach Bake, 123
Pasta-Stuffed Roasted Peppers,
  183
Peanut and Onion Dressing, 101
Peanut-Tofu Stew, 175
Pineapple and Baked Beans Dip,
  157
Pineapple Smoothie, 137
Put Together in Ten Minutes
  Casserole, 77

Quick Tofu Stroganoff, 179
Stuffed Peppers, 93
Tangy Tofu Salad, 64
Tofu (or Seitan or Tempeh) Aztec,
  174
Tofu Scramble, 38

TOMATOES
Balsamic Tomato Soup or Sauce, 98
Brochettes, 162
Multi-Colored Pasta with Broccoli,
  166
Pasta in Paradise, 67
Pasta Now, Pasta Later, 68
Peperonata, 108
Spur of the Moment Salad, 119
Vegetables Provencale, 96
Wonder Gazpacho, 62

TOMATOES, CHOPPED CANNED
Garbanzo-Spinach Curry, 126
Kitchen Sink Minestrone, 59
Quick Cajun Rice and Beans, 81
Zucchini, Green Bean, and Potato
  Stew, 83

TOMATO JUICE
Crank Up the Heat Rice and Beans,
  73

TORTELLINI, VEGAN
Brochettes, 162
Glossary definition, 193

TORTILLA CHIPS
Lemon Tofu and Spinach Bake, 123

TORTILLAS, VEGAN
Baked Beans Quesadillas, 124
Breakfast Potato Burritos, 43
Glossary definition, 193
Potato Tacos, 172

VEGETABLE BROTH
Glossary definition, 194
Vegetable broth recipe, 194

VINEGAR
Low Fat Raspberry Marinade, 106

WALNUTS
Apple Oatmeal, 46
Carrot Orange Cookies, 154
Green and Crunchy Salad, 118
Your Own Granola, 47

WATERMELON
Watermelon Lemonade, 138

WHEAT GERM
Revved-Up Oatmeal, 45

WHITE BEANS
Quick Cajun Rice and Beans, 81

WILD RICE (See rice)

WINE
Ginger and Wine Marinated Fruit, 111
Wild Rice Pilaf with Celery and Carrots, 80

YELLOW SQUASH
Confetti Pasta, 169
Garbs and Carbs, 75
Green and Creamy Soup, 97
Squash on the Barbie, 182

ZUCCHINI
Garbs and Carbs, 75
Green and Creamy Soup, 97
Grilled Veggie Sub, 187
Squash on the Barbie, 182
Vegetables Provencale, 96
Zucchini, Green Bean, and Potato Stew, 83

THIS BOOK IS PRINTED ON RECYCLED PAPER!